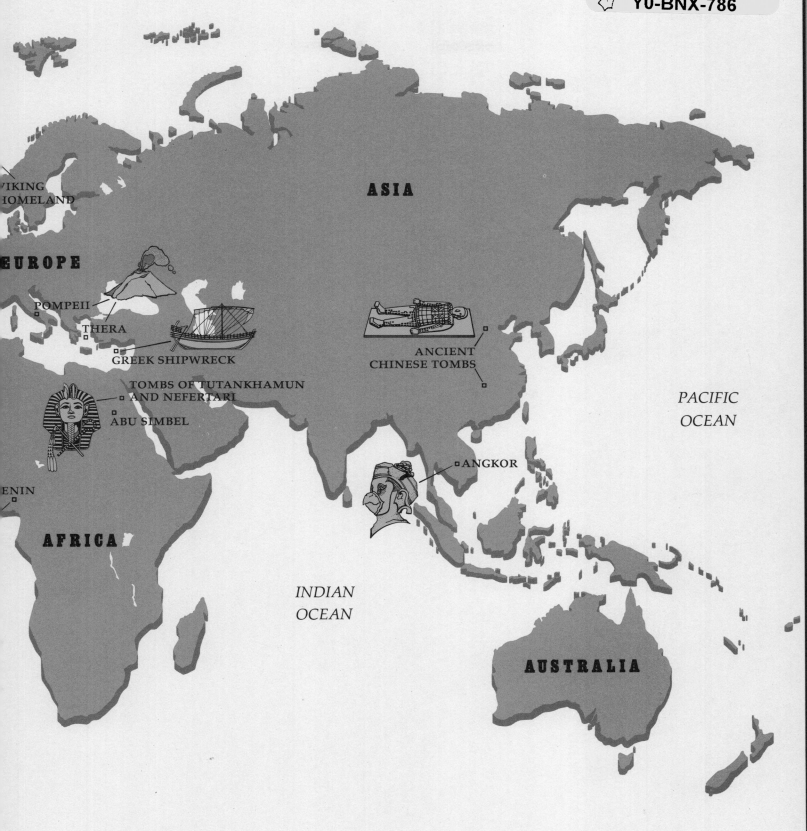

Y0-BNX-786

ASIA

VIKING
HOMELAND

EUROPE

POMPEII

THERA

GREEK SHIPWRECK

ANCIENT
CHINESE TOMBS

TOMBS OF TUTANKHAMUN
AND NEFERTARI

ABU SIMBEL

PACIFIC
OCEAN

ENIN

ANGKOR

AFRICA

INDIAN
OCEAN

AUSTRALIA

A girl holds a Greek jar found in an ancient shipwreck.

SECRETS
FROM THE
PAST

By Gene S. Stuart

☐ BOOKS FOR WORLD EXPLORERS
☐ NATIONAL GEOGRAPHIC SOCIETY

CONTENTS

Huge stones greet the sun at Stonehenge, in England. Ancient people put them there. Read more about this amazing place on page 76.

Copyright © 1979 National Geographic Society
Library of Congress CIP data: page 104

2

1
CAN THE PAST SPEAK TO US?

If these stone lips could talk, they would tell tales of a rich kingdom in Asia, of a great city that lived and died. But stones do not speak. Archaeologists must discover for us the secrets from the past. Archaeologists tell us that this face peering from among twisted roots is a likeness of a king. Once, he ruled a powerful ancient city called Angkor. People in Southeast Asia began building Angkor about 1,000 years ago. They abandoned it 500 years later. Now it lies deserted and in ruins.

Secrets Come from Hidden Tombs

Through many centuries, Egyptians built great tombs for kings and other important people. Inside each tomb, they put things that they thought the buried person might need in the afterlife. As time passed, the locations of many tombs were forgotten. Now, when we discover these burial places, their contents tell us amazing things about how the ancient Egyptians lived.

Gold mask once covered the head and shoulders of King Tutankhamun's mummy. The boy king's tomb, discovered in 1922, was filled with treasures. The tomb of an Egyptian official (right) had more than 30 rooms.

Young Girl Finds Ice Age Paintings!

In 1879, a young Spanish girl named Maria made an exciting discovery. What she found astonished the world. This is her story as she might have told it.

When I woke up that morning, I didn't expect anything special. But soon everything changed. I guess I became famous.

Listen. I'll tell the story once more just for you. I was 9, living here in northern Spain. My papa was Marcelino Sanz de Sautuola.

Papa's hobby was archaeology. He had visited the 1878 World's Fair in Paris and had marveled at new treasures of archaeology.

"Just think, Maria," he said. "I saw animals carved on pieces of bone. Ice Age people made them 16,000 years ago!"

People had found the carvings in French caves. My papa had also found old things in caves. He owns a lot of hilly land around here that has deep caves in it. He digs in them often.

"Today, I plan to spend the whole day digging in the cave I call Altamira," he said. "Come along and help me, if you like, Maria."

He started digging just inside the entrance to the cave. "Look, Maria," he said. "Here are the dark ashes from an ancient campfire. These animal bones and broken shells tell us what food the peo-

Papa took me with him to dig in a cave (left).

ple ate as they huddled around the fire thousands of years ago. And look, here are pieces of old tools made of stone."

As he dug, Papa seemed to forget that I was there. The darkest part of the cave was behind us. I walked a little way into it just for a peek. It didn't seem so dark after all. But the faint light of my lantern made spooky shadows on the stone walls.

"Just a little farther," I said to myself. "I know I can find my way back to Papa." Ahead was a big

In the darkness, I held my lantern high. I saw animals painted on the ceiling (above).

dark hole like a doorway. Beyond it was a huge, long room. I held my lantern high for a better look. Then, suddenly, I saw big red-and-black animals all over the ceiling. I stood amazed, looking at them. When I moved the lantern, they seemed to move. I turned and ran as fast as I could!

"Look, Papa!" I screamed. "Oxen."

"Oxen? Here? What have you seen?" he said.

I led him back to the big room. There, we looked at the animals together. They were not oxen at all.

Papa said they were bison, wild boars, horses, and deer. I'll never forget how excited Papa was.

"They look like the animals I saw carved on the bones," he said. "Maria, do you know what you have found? Some of the Ice Age people must have painted these pictures."

Many more cave paintings have been found in Spain and France. But I discovered the first ones when I was only a little girl. And just imagine! I thought it was going to be an ordinary day.

WHO UNCOVERS ANCIENT SECRETS?

Archaeologists study things of the past and tell us how people once lived. Here, archaeologist Wilhelm Solheim has turned a pot upside down while he carefully fits the broken pieces together. This 5,000-year-old pot came from Southeast Asia.

What Archaeologists Do

All of us, at some time, have found something from the past and wondered about its story. It may have been a piece of an old broken dish. Or it may have been a tiny, rusty wheel that was once part of a machine.

Perhaps we felt curious. We thought: "How did this get here? When was it made? Who owned it? What was it used for?"

Archaeologists also ask questions like these. Archaeologists are scientists who study things left behind by people of the past. They learn to use special tools, and they have years of training to help them find the answers. Sometimes finding answers is like solving a mystery.

Finding the Site

The archaeologist begins by locating a site. A site can be any place where people have lived or left clues. It may be a great city that existed for 1,000 years. Or it may be only a small camp where ancient hunters stopped for a few days and then moved on. Every site, large or small, holds mysteries for archaeologists to solve. "Who were the people who lived here?" archaeologists ask themselves. "What did they look like? What language did they speak? If we could go back in time and spend a day with them, what would it be like?"

To solve the mysteries, the archaeologist must dig into the site and look for clues. An archaeologist is a detective, a scientist, and a reporter. Through archaeology, the past tells its secrets.

Searching for Clues

After an archaeologist decides where to dig, work begins at the site. Sometimes a site is covered with thick plant growth. Bushes and trees must be cleared away. Then the archaeologist makes a map of the site. After the mapping is finished, digging begins. At the end of the digging, marks on the map will show where every artifact was found. An artifact is anything that has been made by people. Archaeologists must read artifacts and other clues the way we read words in a book.

Turn the page to see archaeologists at work at an American Indian site.

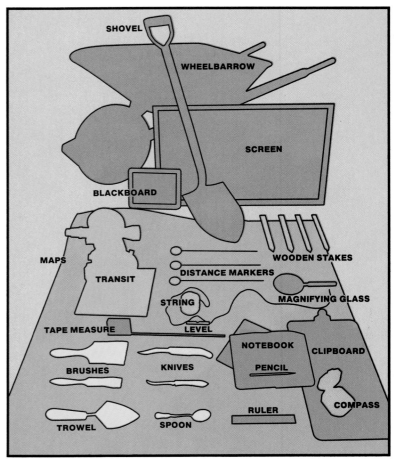

ARCHAEOLOGISTS' TOOLS

1 MEASURING THE SITE	**3** UNCOVERING AND CLEANING
2 DIGGING AND SIFTING	**4** RECORDING THE FINDS

To uncover secrets from the past, archaeologists use many tools. First, they map the site where they plan to dig. They use a compass and a special kind of telescope called a transit to measure the edges of the site accurately. Then, with distance markers, wooden stakes, a level, and string, they make an even grid of squares over the site. This helps them keep records of where things are found. Now they are ready to dig. They shovel dirt into a wheelbarrow and sift the dirt through a screen. The screen traps most small objects. If the archaeologists find a larger object, they uncover it carefully in place, using a trowel, a spoon, or a knife. Then they carefully brush away the dirt. Finally, the archaeologists measure and record everything they find. They publish this information so that others can share it. Turn the page to see these tools in use.

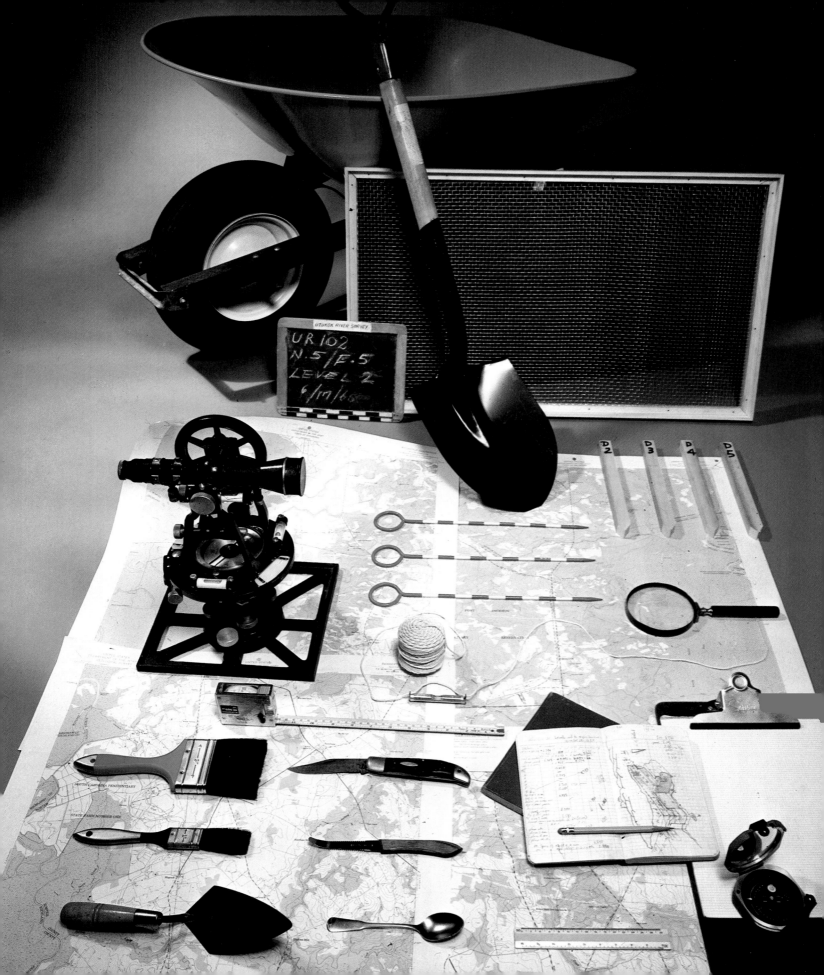

Digging Into the Past

Archaeologists think this mound has secrets to tell. It looks like many Indian mounds in the eastern United States that have yielded clues from the past. But which Indians built this mound? When did they build it? What was their life like? To find answers, archaeologists dig into the past by actually digging into the earth. In fact, while work is going on, a place like the one in this painting is called a dig.

KEEPING RECORDS

Everything that is found gets a number. Workers record when it was found, what spot it came from, and how far down it was. Anything might be a clue telling about the people who lived here.

DIGGING

Often workers dig with picks and shovels first. When they see something they want to save, they switch to small tools such as knives and brushes to avoid damage.

SCREENING

Wheelbarrows bring dirt to be sifted. Seeds and bits of bone found in the dirt show some of the things that the Indians ate.

DISCOVERING WALLS

Dark stains on the ground show where wooden posts have rotted away. They were the walls of a house. The square inside was a cooking hearth.

MAKING PICTURES

A photographer keeps a record by making pictures of every step of the dig from beginning to end. Everything found is photographed.

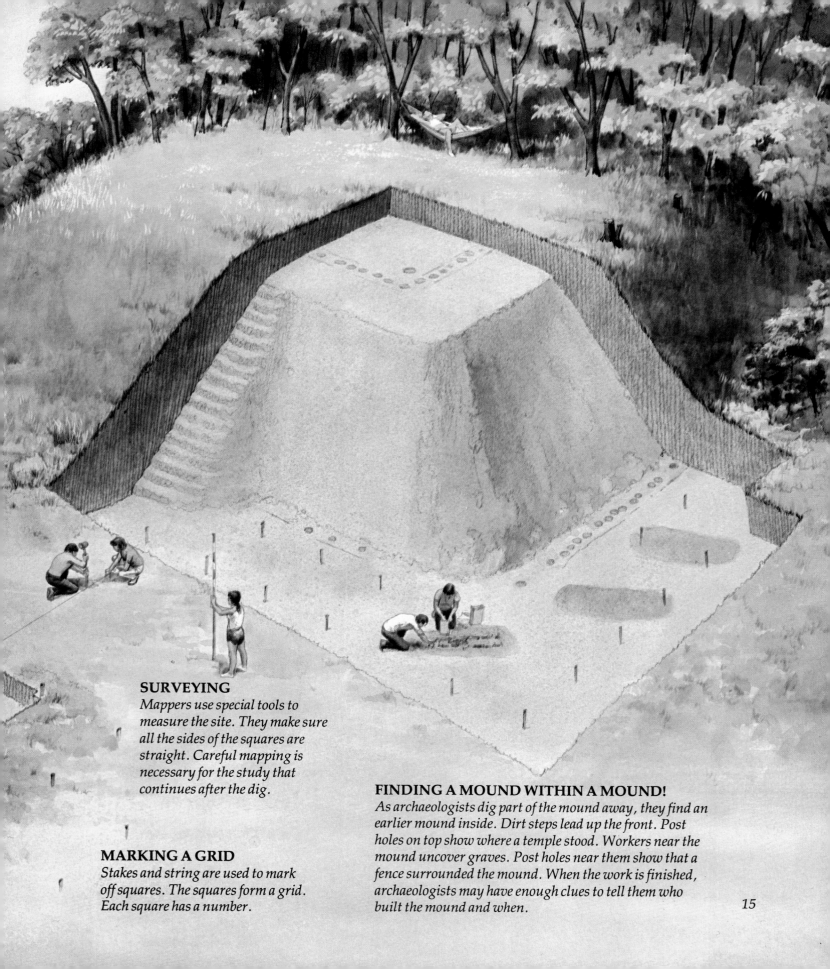

SURVEYING

Mappers use special tools to measure the site. They make sure all the sides of the squares are straight. Careful mapping is necessary for the study that continues after the dig.

MARKING A GRID

Stakes and string are used to mark off squares. The squares form a grid. Each square has a number.

FINDING A MOUND WITHIN A MOUND!

As archaeologists dig part of the mound away, they find an earlier mound inside. Dirt steps lead up the front. Post holes on top show where a temple stood. Workers near the mound uncover graves. Post holes near them show that a fence surrounded the mound. When the work is finished, archaeologists may have enough clues to tell them who built the mound and when.

15

America's Lost City

On these pages, young people are visiting the site of an ancient Indian village. And they are learning how archaeologists study the site. The village was controlled by a great Indian city 20 miles away. Archaeologists call this city Cahokia (say kuh-нон-kee-yuh). No one knows its real name. Nearly 1,000 years ago, about 30,000 people lived in Cahokia. At that time, it was the largest city in what is now the United States.

About 120 dirt mounds were scattered throughout the city. They formed the bases for temples or for the houses of important people. Some mounds were also used as burial places for great leaders.

Archaeologists began digging at Cahokia 100 years ago. Today, modern buildings, parking lots, houses, and superhighways cover much of the site. Only 60 or 70 of the mounds are left.

Thousands of Artifacts

Through the years, archaeologists have found many thousands of artifacts at Cahokia. But digging up artifacts is only the beginning of their work. The archaeologists spend months or even

Viewing the past, students from the Immaculate Conception School in Columbia, Illinois, visit the remains of an ancient village (above). Archaeologist Ann Stahl stands on the floor of an Indian house. She points out holes where wall posts once stood. People today call the village the Range site.

A bucket of dirt can be a treasure to an archaeologist. Ann Stahl carefully lifts a soil sample (right). She dug it from the floor of a house. In a laboratory, other scientists will examine the soil to find out about the Range site people. Bits of wood or straw will tell them what the houses were made of. Seeds, pieces of animal bone, and even pollen from plants will show what foods the people ate. Indian farmers of the Range site probably grew corn and other crops. These crops helped feed the people of the city we call Cahokia.

years studying their finds. Then they report what they have learned.

The unlocked secrets of Cahokia are amazing ones. Rich and powerful priests and chiefs once ruled the city and many villages near the river. The city itself was so large the farmers who lived there could not grow enough food for everyone. So farmers living in smaller villages helped feed Cahokia's thousands of people.

Indians walked long trails and paddled canoes on rivers to bring valuable things to Cahokia. There, archaeologists have uncovered ornaments

Human face on a 1,000-year-old pottery jar may be a clue to what Indians of Cahokia and the Range site looked like. Jewelry may have hung from holes in the ears and forehead of this pot.

With skillful hands (below), Ann Stahl uses an ice pick and a trowel to clear mud from a piece of deer bone.

Once used to store food, this pit later became a place to throw village trash. Archaeologist John C. Arnold and the students found a piece of bone in the pit.

17

made of copper from the Great Lakes area, far to the north. They also found a man buried on a bed of 20,000 beads. The beads were made of seashells from the Gulf of Mexico. This burial told archaeologists that the man had to be a great priest or a powerful chief to lie on such a bed. It also told of trade between Indians living near the Gulf of Mexico and the Indians of Cahokia.

From the top of Monk's Mound, the largest mound at Cahokia, you can see the skyscrapers of St. Louis, Missouri. Today, St. Louis is one of the largest cities in the United States. But once, long ago, the city of Cahokia was *the* largest!

Trees and grass now cover the area around Monk's Mound at Cahokia (below). At right, you can see what the city looked like many centuries ago.

Students inspect a map of the past. Indians lived at the Range site four different times. Archaeologist John Kelly shows where houses stood 1,000 years ago. Indians first came to this site 4,000 years ago.

Prehistoric Cahokia comes alive in an artist's painting. After years of digging, archaeologists can tell us about the city. Trading canoes traveled the rivers. A wall of posts protected Cahokia from enemies. Temples stood on Monk's Mound in the center. The huge mound is as tall as a ten-story building.

Sites Beneath the Sea

Did the small Greek ship plunge out of control on a dark, stormy sea? Or did it make a desperate run for shore, trying to get away from pirates? No one can be sure. But archaeologists know that the ship went down less than a mile from the island of Cyprus. It slowly settled onto the seafloor, 90 feet below the surface. There it lay for more than 2,200 years. Finally, a Greek diver found it and led archaeologists to the site.

The ship was a trading vessel with a captain and a crew of three. It carried as its cargo jars of wine and stones for grinding grain into flour.

How do we know so much about something that happened so long ago? Archaeologists found things that tell the story. Grinding stones and more than 400 wine jars lay in the wreckage. Archaeologists can tell when the jars were made. So they know about when the ship sank.

Almonds, carried as food for the crew, still lay in heaps. The sacks that once held them had rotted. The divers found dishes and spoons for four. So they know how many people lived on board and something about their meals.

Only a few coins were found in the wreck, and the ship's wooden sides were scarred by metal spear points. This makes archaeologists suspect a pirate attack and robbery!

Underwater archaeology is very different from archaeology on land. In both cases, archaeologists measure and record everything. But artifacts underwater are usually clues to a disaster. They show us one moment of the past instead of a picture of life in one place over many years.

Both land and sea archaeology let us touch the past with our own hands.

An ancient Greek trading ship, shown in the painting at right, sank to the bottom of the Mediterranean Sea more than 2,200 years ago. It is one of the oldest sunken ships ever found. Mud on the bottom of the sea preserved the wooden hull. The mud also preserved thousands of almonds the ship carried. After measuring and recording the wreck site, archaeologists brought up the planks. Then they put the ship back together. On the opposite page, a diver lifts a wine jar. The cargo included more than 400 jars of wine.

Almonds still in their shells (above) were found at the ancient wreck. Capturing the past, an artist draws pottery dishes (left). They once held food and drink for the captain and crew.

Squirrel fish swims among broken pottery
jars found on the seafloor near Cyprus.

3

HOW DID WE GET HERE TODAY?

People have moved from one place to another for many reasons. Early hunters wandered in search of big game. Some people hoped to find riches and adventure. The ancestors of the children in this picture sailed great distances over the Pacific Ocean as they looked for new island homes.

How Did We Get Here Today?

Voke Leaves His Island in Search of a New Home

If a boy like Voke (say VOH-kay) had lived on one of the Polynesian islands a thousand years ago, he might have migrated to another island. This is the story of such a journey as Voke might have told it to his children.

Many years ago, when I was a young boy, I lived on another island. It was a long way from here. I still remember the good times I had! I climbed the mountains and swam in the streams.

But some things about the island were not good. It was crowded with too many people. Sometimes there was not enough food for everyone. Although our island was small, it had two chiefs. Some people followed one chief, some obeyed the other.

One day my father said to me, "Voke, we must

my little sister and our dog, and we boarded our canoe. Soon, our canoe and the two others were little dots on the great sea.

My father guided the canoe as we sailed using the signs of the sea. The shapes and movements of clouds told him islands were near. Birds flying home at sunset pointed the way to land. Different colors in the water meant that we were near or far away from land. "I feel with my body the rise and fall of the waves," he told me. "I know which islands the waves come from. By day, the sun also guides me. At night, I follow the stars."

One night a great storm came. We could not see the stars. Heavy wind and rain swept down upon us. Yet my father stayed in the navigator's place in the canoe, and I stayed with him.

"During storms, we cannot see the signs and sometimes lose our way," he said. All through that night and the next day, the storm raged. As darkness closed upon us again, the rain stopped. The wind died. We saw bright stars once more. My father turned the canoe toward a star on the horizon.

"Look," he said. "That is the way. The god of the sea guided us through the storm. Now, once more, we will sail along the path of the stars."

So we followed the stars and sea signs for many nights and days. And that is how we came to our new island where no one had lived before us.

Leaving our island (at left), we took things we would need in our new home. My father guided our canoe by watching the heavens and the signs of the sea.

leave our home. Many people want to go away to another island with our chief and begin a new life. We will go with them."

The men prepared three canoes large enough for almost 100 people. The women packed food for a long journey. The children rounded up pigs and chickens. I made cages for the chickens out of sticks and vines. All of us gathered young plants and seeds to put into the soil of our new land.

Very early one morning, my mother woke me. "Come, Voke," she whispered. "It is time." I got

People of Many Islands

Where did the people of the Pacific islands come from? How did they find their way around the ocean from island to island? Until a few years ago, the answers were a mystery. Now we have clues to help us unlock the secret of their journeys.

The first people to reach the Pacific islands came from Southeast Asia. At first, they settled on islands near the mainland. Then, over thousands of years, they spread eastward across the ocean.

Some settled a large group of islands in the Pacific Ocean called Polynesia (say pahl-uh-NEE-zhuh).

For at least 2,000 years, brave navigators like Tevake, who sailed his outrigger canoe until 1970, have roamed the Pacific Ocean. The vessel was much like those his ancestors used. Dancers on an island in Polynesia (right) celebrate the story of their land's discovery by Ru, an ancient navigator.

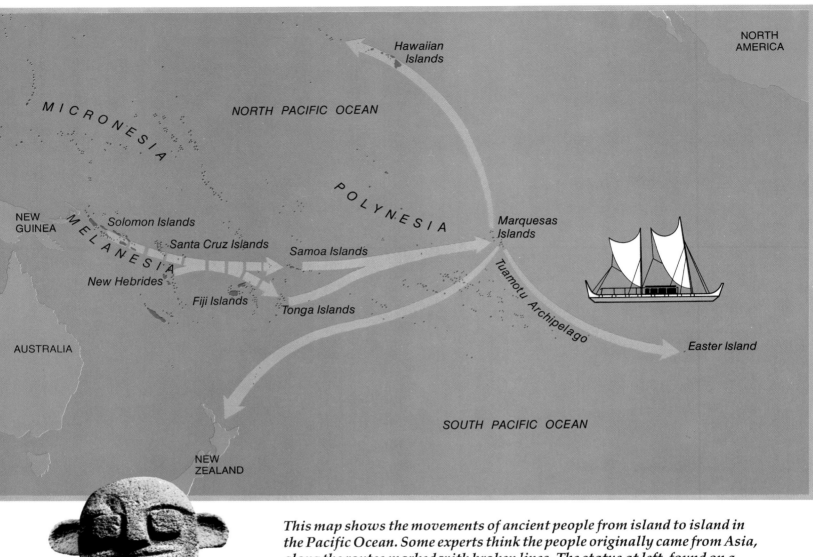

This map shows the movements of ancient people from island to island in the Pacific Ocean. Some experts think the people originally came from Asia, along the routes marked with broken lines. The statue at left, found on a Hawaiian island, resembles statues from islands 3,000 miles away.

Packed for a voyage: Fruits, nuts, dried fish, gourds of water, and foods packaged in leaves fed islanders on trips that lasted for weeks.

The word Polynesia means "many islands." When the people settled in a new place, they often made clay pottery, and tools of stone and bone. These pots and tools were much like those they had made in their old location. Finding similar things in two or more places suggests that people with similar customs made them. From studying things people left behind, archaeologists can tell something about when and where the people traveled, and how they found their way.

When the people set out on long journeys, they took animals and plants with them so they would have food in their new land. These plants and animals provide more clues to their travels. Some of the same kinds of plants and animals live on the islands today. Other clues are religious customs, languages, living habits, and old stories.

Men and women who remembered the journeys often told the children about them. Older navigators told younger ones how to find their way across the sea in large sailing canoes. Even today, some men know how to sail by using the old ways.

To experts, these skills and stories can be like the pages of a history book.

The First Americans Arrive

Have you ever thought about the American Indians and wondered where they came from? The name sounds as if they came from India. But they didn't. When Columbus returned from the New World, he announced that he had reached the Indies, islands off the coast of Asia. He called the people he saw Indians.

Explorers who came later, however, knew that North and South America were new lands, their people previously unknown to Europeans. As stories about America's "Indians" spread through Europe, people began trying to find answers to puzzling questions.

"Who are these unknown people?" they asked. "How did they get where they are?"

Many Europeans believed the earliest Indians had come to America in boats. "But where did the Indians come from?" they wondered. Some people guessed that the Indians had come from Europe or Africa. Many believed they had come from an imaginary continent called Atlantis.

Which of these answers was correct? Probably none of them. Scientists believe that the Indians

The bridge of land that connected Asia to North America during the Ice Age was more than 1,000 miles wide in some places (below).

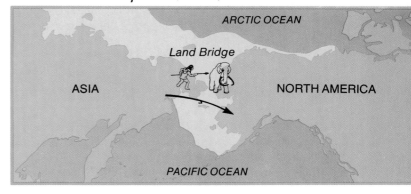

In the painting at left, Ice Age hunters butcher a woolly mammoth. Some people cut meat into big slabs. Others put some of the pieces in a storage pit, at far left, to save them for later use. Two people build a shelter. When they killed a large animal, hunters probably camped nearby until they had taken everything they could use.

31

During the Ice Age, large beasts roamed a plain that connected Asia to North America. Ice Age people hunted some animals, such as a kind of camel that is now extinct and the giant sloth. The people feared other, fiercer animals, including the lionlike cat. All of these animals died out long ago.

are descendants of people who came from Asia. Some may have traveled along the coast in small boats. But most probably walked across on dry land. Some scientists believe these people began their long walk during the last Ice Age—perhaps as early as 40,000 years ago. At that time, a thick layer of ice covered northern parts of what are now North America and Asia. So much water was frozen that oceans were shallower than they are now. More land was exposed. A strip of land more than 1,000 miles wide joined Asia and North America. This wide strip is often called the land bridge.

The land bridge was a huge plain. Thick grass and bushes grew there. At that time, herds of large animals such as mammoths, giant moose, and musk-oxen roamed Asia and North America. In their constant search for food, many of the animals gradually wandered onto the land bridge. Some finally crossed it.

Following the Herds

The Ice Age people of Asia probably followed herds of animals to North America. These people lived by hunting. They ate the meat of the animals they killed and used the furs and skins for clothing and shelters. Sharpened animal bones became useful tools and weapons.

The human figures outlined above show the size of typical Ice Age people compared to some of the large animals of their time.

Ice Age hunters lived in small groups called bands. If a band killed a large animal, the members of the group might have enough meat for weeks. The people probably built shelters somewhat like tents near their kill. The hunters may have built a framework of large animal bones and stretched animal hides over it.

Slowly, animals and people moved from Asia to North America. When the animals stopped, the people stopped also. When the animals moved on again, the people followed. They never knew they were crossing from Asia into North America. They were simply living from day to day.

These people became the first Americans. When

TOOLS AND WEAPONS

Indians made stone spear points like the one above 12,000 years ago. Using ancient methods, Elizabeth Hawkins, 10, of Arlington, Virginia, learns to shape a scraping tool (below). She and archaeologist Dennis Stanford wear protective goggles.

This double-edged scraper is made of obsidian, or volcanic glass. Ice Age hunters may have made such a scraper 35,000 years ago. Stanford made this one, using stone and antler tools like those used by Ice Age people.

they arrived, they found many kinds of animals in the Americas. No people had ever lived here before. It took thousands of years for the Asian people and their descendants to spread over all of North and South America.

The people kept hunting wild animals. Mammoths and other large beasts became scarce and finally died out. But the hunters continued to find plenty of smaller game. Some people stayed in the cold areas. Others gradually moved farther south. Eventually, some traveled all the way to the southern tip of South America—more than 10,000 miles from the land bridge!

Scientists think all American Indians, no matter how much some tribes may differ from others, are descended from people who originally came from Asia. Some groups continued to depend on hunting. Others lived by fishing or by gathering wild plants. Much later, some learned how to farm.

How do we know all this when it happened so many years ago? Archaeologists have dug up tools used by ancient people in North America and Asia. They have found spear points the hunters left behind. Animal bones made into tools give clues to the time when the first people may have crossed the land bridge. Other sites all over the Americas show where Indians lived, when they lived there, and how they lived.

European explorers wondered where the Indians came from. But archaeologists today have solved at least part of the mystery, and the search for more answers goes on.

Modern equipment helps an Indian high school girl in Mississippi improve her language skills. Experts now believe that people who came from Asia to North America during the Ice Age were ancestors of all the American Indians.

An Indian boy dresses in bright feathers and beads to take part in a tribal fair in Montana (above). Indians in New Mexico (right) whirl in a colorful dance. Many Indian customs, dances, and costumes go back hundreds of years.

Vikings Sail the Seas

Viking ships coming! Just to hear these words struck terror into the heart. Beginning about 1,200 years ago, and continuing for more than 250 years, the Vikings swept out of the north into richer parts of Europe. Everyone feared the fierce sea raiders.

The ships of the Vikings were small and swift. They could sail inland on rivers or cross wide oceans. Viking warriors attacked towns and cities everywhere. They carried away gold and other treasure. Often they burned settlements after seizing everything of value. When the robbing and killing were over, they sailed home with their riches.

At first, the Vikings robbed and destroyed everywhere. But when they went back to settlements to steal again, the people often had nothing valuable left. The Vikings finally found that they would be better off using their ships for commerce. Through the years, they changed from raiders to traders.

Their trade routes took them as far south as North Africa. Rivers led them deep into Europe. The map on this page shows some of the places where Vikings traveled and settled. Areas of Britain and France became parts of Viking kingdoms. Settlers from the northlands moved there. York, England, served as one trading center. It became a busy city with thousands of people.

Some Vikings went east. They founded cities

Garrett Bourque, 11, of Jefferson, Maine, examines a 900-year-old Viking silver coin with his father. The coin, shown enlarged at right, was found at an Indian village site in Maine. Archaeologists think the coin may have been traded to Indians there by Indians from Newfoundland.

Eyes alert for enemies and weapons ready for battle, a young Viking warrior keeps watch in the painting at left. He patrols a wall built of earth and logs. The wall protected trade routes and kept enemies from invading. Vikings once ruled territory in northern Europe from England to Russia.

Viking explorers searched the seas for new lands to colonize. Sailing westward, they settled Iceland and then Greenland. The first European to see America may have been Bjarni Herjulfsson, a Viking sea captain lost in a storm. Leif Ericsson, another Viking captain, probably landed on the coast of what is now Newfoundland.

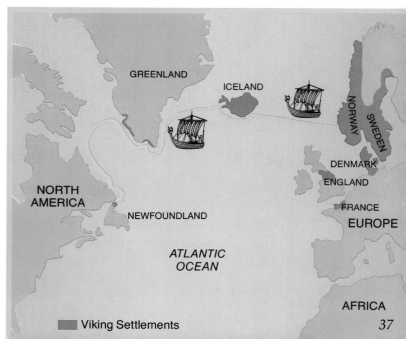

Viking Settlements

37

Viking ships have come home! In this painting, excited villagers hurry to the beach to greet adventurers returning from the sea. Ships sailed from villages like this one to raid other lands. Later, the Vikings became traders and settlers.

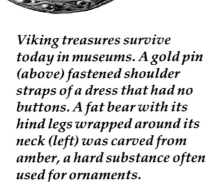

Viking treasures survive today in museums. A gold pin (above) fastened shoulder straps of a dress that had no buttons. A fat bear with its hind legs wrapped around its neck (left) was carved from amber, a hard substance often used for ornaments.

along rivers in what later became Russia. Others sailed west, far into the Atlantic Ocean.

At that time, most Europeans believed horrible monsters lurked at the edge of the earth, waiting to gobble up people who came too close. But the fearless Vikings sailed beyond the horizon and discovered Iceland and Greenland.

Some went even farther and landed on the conti-nent of North America. A Viking sea captain named Leif Ericsson probably was the first European to land in the New World. Five hundred years before Columbus, Ericsson spent the winter at a place he called Vinland. Most experts think it was somewhere in what is now Newfoundland.

About a century later, Viking ships returned to America carrying 160 settlers. They founded a

Straining at the oars, Danish Boy Scouts row a copy of a Viking longship. The Scouts built this ship and five others. They shaped the wood with copies of Viking tools. Then they put the ship together, using construction methods much like those of the Vikings. The finished ship had 32 oars, plus sails.

small colony in Vinland. There, a boy named Snorri Karlsefni was born. He was the first child born to European colonists in the Americas.

Archaeologists have discovered the remains of the Viking settlement where Snorri may have been born. Outlines of houses are still there. The archaeologists have found such things as a metal pin and a tool for spinning yarn.

A mother in a Viking colony dresses her child. An old Viking story tells about this boy, Snorri Karlsefni. Snorri was born in what was probably the first Viking settlement in North America. The small colony failed after three years.

Most Viking history was in the form of stories told by word of mouth. One such story told of Snorri and his family living for a while in a land west of Greenland. So when archaeologists found the village in Newfoundland, they not only learned that the Vikings had sailed to America long before Columbus, they also discovered that some of the old stories were based on truth.

Putting to sea under full sail like their Viking ancestors, Boy Scouts in Denmark relive the past (right). The ship is an exact copy of one archaeologists dug up in Denmark. Fast ships helped Vikings raid Europe for treasure.

4

LOST CITIES: ABANDONED AND FORGOTTEN

Chipped stone faces gaze from the crumbling walls and towers of Angkor. Once this was the capital of an empire in Southeast Asia. What happened to make people suddenly leave Angkor and other "forgotten" cities?

Tilaka Flees Her Home

Angkor was a powerful city in Southeast Asia. In this story, a woman named Tilaka (say tee-LAH-kuh) tells her granddaughter about a battle at Angkor in 1431.

Watch me closely, Granddaughter. Push the roots of the rice plants into the mud. Give each plant in our small field room to grow. Long ago, there were rice fields as far as one could see. I lived beyond the mountains then, in a splendid city. It had a high wall and four carved stone gates. The king was so wealthy his palace had a tall golden tower. My father was a rich man. We had a large house and many servants. When I

Here we live by growing rice, and we have peace.

danced in the temple with other young girls, I wore a costume of red silk and a headdress of gold.

But when I was about your age, something terrible happened. Our enemies had made war on us for many months. Thousands of soldiers, some riding horses or elephants, surrounded the city. The farmers could not harvest the rice.

One day, my father called me and said, "A big battle is coming, Tilaka. Our soldiers cannot win. We must flee for our lives." Our servants filled our horse cart with gold, silk, and china. My mother and I put on our jewelry and tried to cover it with our clothes. Mother put my gold hairpin in my hair. I picked up my cat and climbed into the cart.

As we left the city, soldiers seemed to be everywhere. Some rode horses. Princes rode war ele-

Father lifted me up, and mother pulled me onto an elephant. My brother ran beside it as we fled the city.

phants. The king's bodyguard of 100 strong, beautiful women surrounded him as he stood on his elephant holding his gold sword. Spears and arrows flew through the air. Terrible new weapons called cannons boomed like thunder. Most of our servants screamed and ran as a cannonball killed our horse. I saw our city on fire.

Then a boy servant stopped a royal war elephant that had broken from the rest. My father lifted my mother and me onto it. My older brother ran alongside. We left the city and did not stop until we were far away. We traveled south for many days, until we came to this place. Since then, we have lived as rice farmers. Sometimes, when I wear my gold hairpin, I think about the city of my childhood and the things that happened there so long ago.

Stone walkway leads to Angkor (say ANG-kor) in Southeast

The Silent City

This stone crocodile was carved on a wall at Angkor. Once, crocodiles helped protect the city. They lived in water-filled moats around the walls.

46

"Who built this place?" The Frenchman asked the question again and again. The people he asked did not know the answer. "The king of angels," said one. "It is the work of the giants," said another.

The Frenchman was a scholar named Henri Mouhot. He went to what is now Kampuchea (say kahm-POOCH-ee-ah) more than a hundred years ago. This nation used to be called Cambodia.

While Mouhot was there, he heard stories of a lost city. So he set out to find it. At last, after cutting through thick forest and wading across muddy

Asia. For centuries, forest plants hid this ancient city from the world.

Headdress of a dancer looks much like those worn by dancers in an ancient carving (above).

Part man, part bird, the Garuda (say guh-ROO-duh) served a god of Angkor. This Garuda was found in the ancient city.

swamps, he found the city he was looking for. He wrote, ". . . hardly a sound echoes but the roar of tigers, the shrill trumpeting of elephants."

Mouhot found writing on the temple walls. Many years later, archaeologists learned how to read this writing. It told them something about the ancient city of Angkor.

For 500 years, Angkor was the capital of a large empire. At one time, about a million people lived in the capital. Then enemies invaded, and the people fled. Now partly restored, the buildings of Angkor reveal their stories of the past.

Fleeing for their lives, people of Thera crowd into boats and sail away from their island home. The volcano on

Thera erupted about 3,500 years ago. It almost destroyed the island. The volcanic eruption was one of

48

the largest in history. It covered the island with a thick layer of ash.

An Island Explodes

On a little island known as Thera, the earth began to shake. Stone houses broke apart and tumbled into the streets. The volcano at the center of the island was erupting!

Several small eruptions during the past weeks had frightened the people of Thera. But this disaster was far more terrible. A huge explosion blew the fiery heart out of the volcano, and the top caved in! The center of the island disappeared, leaving a hole that is now a deep part of the Aegean Sea near the coast of Greece.

Digging in the part of the island that did not vanish 3,500 years ago, archaeologists recently uncovered the narrow streets of a town. They found houses with brightly painted walls. But they did not find skeletons or valuables. They think the people had time to pack and escape. Some experts believe the Thera disaster gave rise to a famous story—the legend of the lost continent of Atlantis.

Restoring the past, an expert fills in missing pieces of a wall painting from a house on Thera. The picture shows two boys boxing.

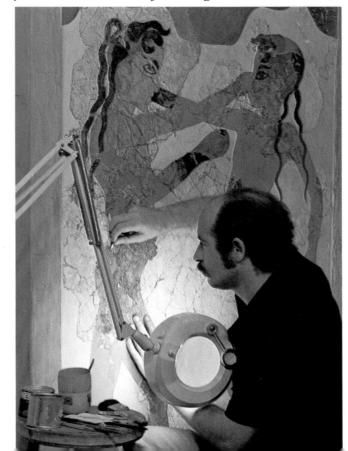

The Darkest Day

In ancient times, the Bay of Naples was a favorite place for wealthy Romans to spend summer vacations. They escaped the city heat and enjoyed the cool breezes.

A teenage Roman boy called Pliny (say PLIH-nee) the Younger was visiting his uncle there on an August day 1,900 years ago. As Pliny looked across the bay, he saw something frightening. A gigantic cloud rose into the sky. Pliny later described the cloud in a letter: "At one moment it was white, at another dark and dirty, as if it carried up a load of earth and cinders."

What Pliny saw was the eruption of the volcano called Vesuvius. Although it was morning, the sky turned completely black as the force of the eruption sent rock and ash flying into the air. The debris rained down on the city of Pompeii, at the foot of the volcano. Many residents ran for their lives and escaped unharmed. But many more were trapped and buried by the falling debris.

Three days later, when the sky cleared, most of Pompeii was buried in 20 feet of volcanic rock and ash. Through the years, people forgot the exact

Shielding their heads from debris, people of Pompeii try to escape during the eruption of Vesuvius.

location of this Roman city. Then, about 230 years ago, farmers working above Pompeii discovered some of the ruins.

Later, archaeologists uncovered streets, houses, theaters, and shops. The deep ash had preserved wall paintings and statues. Houses of the wealthy still held jewelry and dishes of gold and silver. Posters announced an election of city officials. The archaeologists even found a table set for breakfast. Eggs, bread, figs, and nuts lay ready to eat.

Pompeii is a rare and valuable site. Few ruins have as many things so well preserved. Uncovering Pompeii is like bringing a city to life again—a city where time suddenly stopped.

Carefully reconstructing the past, a workman pours plaster into one of many holes found at Pompeii (above). Later, he will scrape the volcanic ash away, and discover that the plaster has hardened into the shape of a human being. Some victims of the Vesuvius eruption were covered by ash. Over many years the ash hardened. When the bodies decayed, holes were left in the ash. Plaster poured into these "molds" now shows the people just as they fell.

Plaster copies of bodies (left) lie near the gates of Pompeii. These people died trying to flee the city. Some who left earlier escaped. Using plaster, archaeologists at Pompeii have also made copies of food, furniture, and even dogs. At times, the shapes of sandals and folds of clothing show clearly. One dog wore a collar with studs.

51

Rangers at Mesa Verde (say MAY-suh VAIR-deh) National Park in Colorado lead visitors through Cliff Palace (above). It included sleeping rooms, storage areas, and places to hold ceremonies.

Smoke rises as a woman carries food down a ladder to men in an underground room called a kiva (say KEE-vuh). Indians used circular kivas like the one in the painting at left as gathering places, for religious ceremonies, and as workshops.

Pueblo Indians at Taos, New Mexico, live in houses made of mud and stone (right), the same materials used to build Cliff Palace.

Indian Cliff Dwellers

Some of the cattle had strayed away, and now they were lost! Two young cowboys saddled their horses and pushed through the snows of Mesa Verde in search of them. Miles later, they stopped and stared in wonder.

Across a deep canyon, they saw a city! It was half hidden on a ledge partway up a cliff. The year was 1888, and the cowboys were looking at the lost city we now call Cliff Palace.

Indian farmers lived at Cliff Palace, in what is now Colorado, 800 years ago. Archaeologists believe the city was the home of more than 200 people. Suddenly, they all moved, leaving pottery and other possessions scattered through the city.

Over the years, scientists have tried to solve the mystery of why the Indians left and where they went. They found a clue in the trunks of trees! Rings that form each year as trees grow showed a long drought about 700 years ago. The rings during that period were narrow, because the trees had little water for growth. The dry time may have caused the people to move to places where there was more water. Pueblo Indians living today in New Mexico and Arizona make the same kinds of baskets and pottery found at Cliff Palace. They build homes of the same materials. So archaeologists believe these Indians are probably descendants of the cliff dwellers.

Archaeology students from the University of Colorado measure a jar found near Cliff Palace. Such jars were used to store food and water.

53

Mountaintop Secret

Nearly 70 years ago, an American professor named Hiram Bingham went to the Andes, high mountains in the western part of South America. There, Bingham hoped to find the ruins of buildings used by the Indians of Peru long ago. As he traveled through the forest, he met an Indian man. Bingham asked the Indian if he knew of any ruins. "Yes," the man replied, and pointed straight up a huge mountain.

The man agreed to lead Bingham to the ruins. They set off in a cold drizzle. They struggled through the forest and up a long slope. To climb the steepest places, they had to use logs with notches cut in them as ladders. One slip would have sent them tumbling down the side of the mountain into the fast-moving river below.

They climbed for two hours. Then they saw two men and a boy working in small fields cut into the

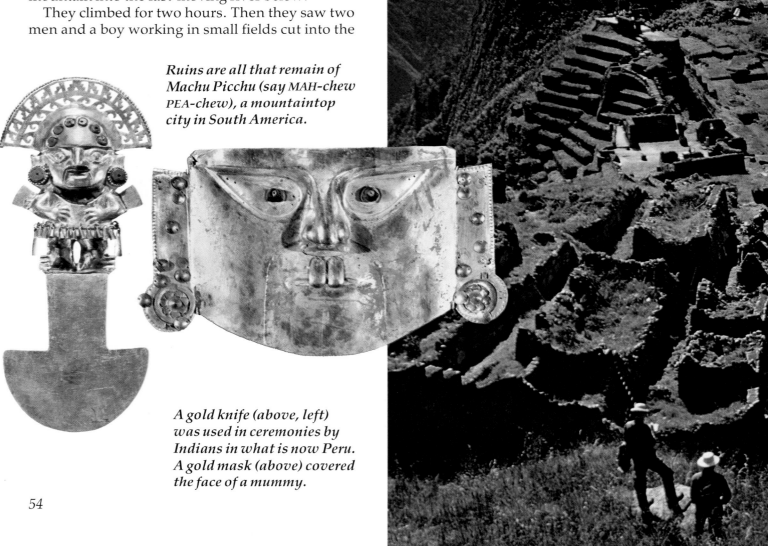

Ruins are all that remain of Machu Picchu (say MAH-chew PEA-chew), a mountaintop city in South America.

A gold knife (above, left) was used in ceremonies by Indians in what is now Peru. A gold mask (above) covered the face of a mummy.

mountainside. The boy led Bingham to a deserted city between two mountain peaks. In the city, Bingham saw the ruins of a large staircase, a temple, and many houses. All were made of stones tightly fitted together. He found an altar to the sun god and a fountain that had once provided water.

Bingham had reached a lost Inca (say ING-kuh) city. We now call it Machu Picchu. Centuries ago, the city was part of the Inca empire. This huge empire began as a small Indian kingdom in the mountains of what is now Peru. Inca armies conquered other groups of Indians until, finally, the mighty Inca empire stretched up and down much of the west coast of South America.

To hold their empire together, Inca rulers needed a good communications system. Their soldiers had to be able to move from place to place quickly. So the Incas built a network of highways. Many

Leaders of the Inca empire chose certain girls to serve the sun god. When the girls were about 8, they went to live in special houses. There, they learned cooking and fine weaving. After they grew up, many married rulers or nobles.

Indian pots took many shapes, including a parrot, a fish, and a head. They were made by craftsmen conquered by the Incas.

The work of Indian potters has stood the test of time. Ashley Goodrich, 12, of Fairview, Pennsylvania, pours water from a jar more than 400 years old.

were paved with stone. Messengers from all parts of the empire ran along these roads, bringing news to the leaders. The leaders needed many workers to build and repair their roads and their forts and cities. They made a law that every man had to work part of each year for the empire. In return, people received help when times were hard. The rulers filled storehouses with food for those in need.

By the time Columbus arrived in the New World, the Incas were the most powerful Indians in the Americas. Then, in 1532, Spanish gold-seekers came to the Inca empire with guns and horses. They took the emperor prisoner and held him for a huge ransom—more than 24 tons of gold and silver! After they got the ransom, the Spaniards killed the emperor and took over the empire.

When Bingham saw Machu Picchu, he thought perhaps it had been built high in the mountains as a hideout from the Spaniards. As archaeologists studied the city, they realized it was built before the Spanish army came. They believe it was once a fortress and a place where religious ceremonies were held. But they don't think Spanish conquerors ever discovered Machu Picchu. It remained hidden from the world for centuries, until a young Indian boy led Bingham to it.

Tiny gold llama (say YAH-muh) came from a tomb in Peru. Llamas carried Inca burdens and provided wool.

Indian men and a llama cross Lake Titicaca. Their reed boat is like those used long ago.

58   *Musicians perform, and actors in costume represent gods. This painting is a copy of one found*

Forest Hides Maya Cities

Great cities once dotted the land of the Maya (say MY-yuh). It stretched from what is now southern Mexico to Honduras in Central America.

Rulers and priests lived in grand palaces. Temples, painted bright red or blue, stood tall in the tropical sunlight. Crowds of people filled the busy cities. Some shopped at markets that sold everything from bowls of food to pet parrots.

Then, the Maya began leaving many of their large cities. They scattered through the countryside to live in small villages or on farms. Why? What could have happened?

Archaeologists can only guess. Some believe the

Mist rises from the ruins of Palenque (say pah-LENG-kay), an ancient Maya city in Mexico (left). The pyramid on the right holds the tomb of a ruler.

Archaeologists study a ruined temple at Tancah (say tahn-KAH), Mexico (below). Only parts of the stone roof are still in place. Thick tree roots often hold crumbling walls like this one together.

in Bonampak (say bone-ahm-PAHK) in Mexico.

59

people grew angry at the rulers and priests and rebelled against them. Others say terrible disease may have killed thousands of people. Many experts think that crops failed and that lack of food drove the Maya from their homes.

The large cities crumbled. Slowly trees and other forest plants grew in a tangle over the buildings. Through the years, the Maya forgot about many of the splendid cities of their ancestors. Finally, after centuries had passed, archaeologists found some of these hidden ruins.

Scientists and explorers are still discovering temples and whole cities. A discovery made about 30 years ago is one of the most exciting.

Deep in the Mexican forest and miles from the nearest village, a ruined Maya city had been found. A photographer named Giles Healey decided to go there and make documentary films. He hired several Maya Indian men as guides.

Soon after they arrived, the men saw a deer and set out after it with a rifle. A few minutes later, they came running back, shouting excitedly, "Come, you must see what we have found."

The Lost Temple

Healey followed them to a small temple. It was so thickly covered with plants that no one had noticed it before. He went inside. Brightly colored paintings of Maya people completely filled the walls and ceiling of a small room.

He had to hack bushes away to enter the next room. "When I stepped in, a big black cat, a puma, stepped out. If it had been a female with young, it would have killed me," he said. Healey saw that the second room also had paintings on the walls and ceiling. So did the third.

The little temple is like a time capsule of Maya history. One painting shows warriors in a battle. Another shows prisoners being led before a ruler. On one of the walls, musicians (see pages 58 and 59) parade past actors in costume. On other walls, priests and members of the royal court are dressed for a ceremony. Finally, the ceremony itself is shown. A man holds up a young child. The child will be the next ruler of the city.

Archaeologists have named the city Bonampak. In Maya, the word means "dyed walls."

The 1,200-year-old walls have told their story. But many more cities may lie undiscovered in the forest. They are waiting to tell their secrets, too.

Maya sun god holds the attention of archaeologist David Sedat. The sun god was one of the most important Maya gods. Sedat's hands rest on a giant ear ornament and a huge necklace. This carving decorates a temple wall in Guatemala.

Moonlight and clouds streak the sky above Chichen Itza (say chee-CHEHN eetz-AH) in Mexico (right). Priests may have used this building as an observatory. Studying the heavens helped them decide when special events should take place.

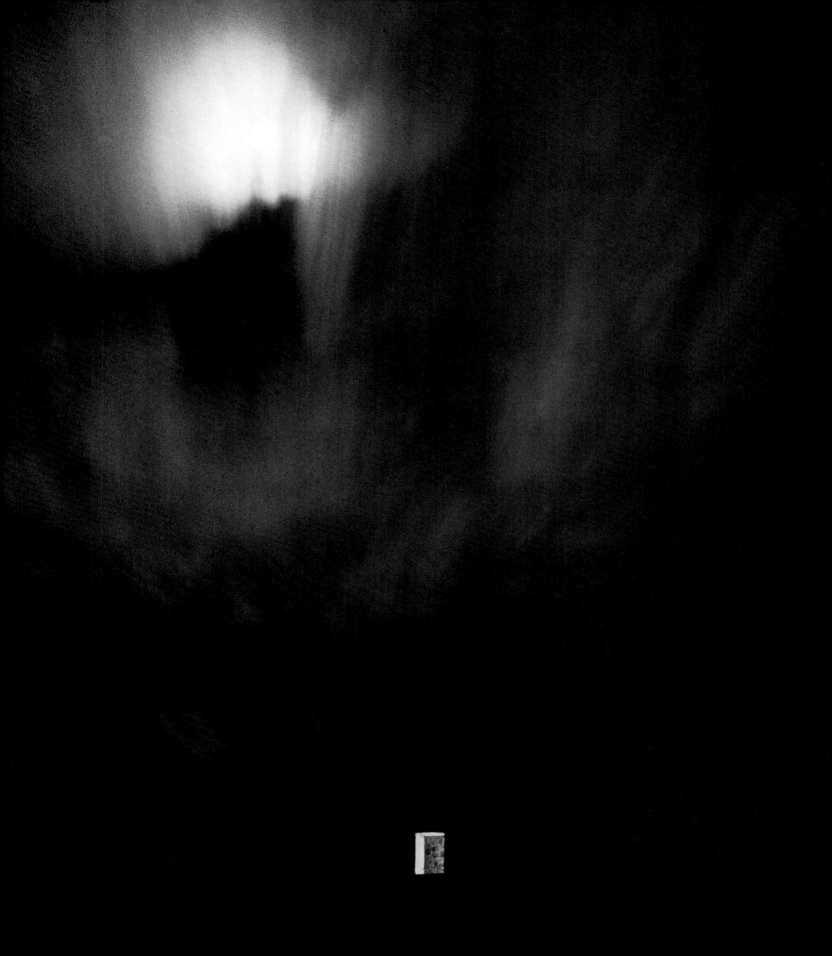

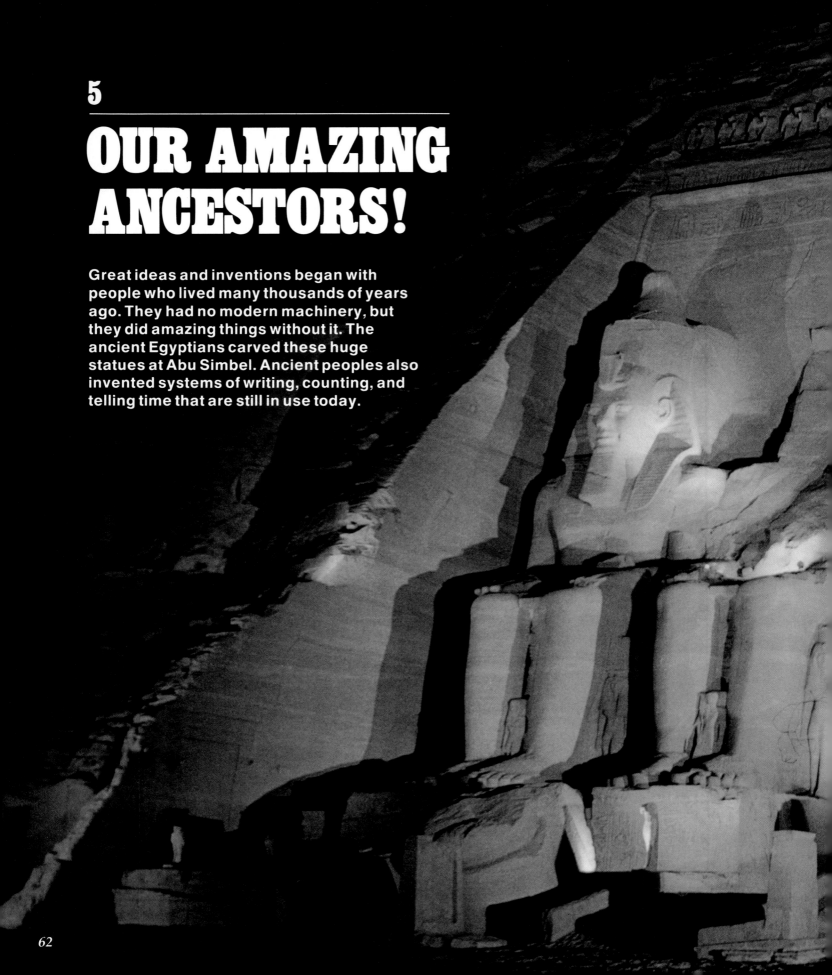

5

OUR AMAZING ANCESTORS!

Great ideas and inventions began with people who lived many thousands of years ago. They had no modern machinery, but they did amazing things without it. The ancient Egyptians carved these huge statues at Abu Simbel. Ancient peoples also invented systems of writing, counting, and telling time that are still in use today.

Hui Meets a Master Artist

An artist named Hui (say WHO-ee) lived in ancient Egypt when King Ramesses II ruled with his favorite queen, Nefertari. This is a story about something that could have happened to Hui when he was a young boy.

Oh, Mother! Hear what I have to say. I ran as fast as I could across the hot sand to tell you. I cannot believe it happened to me! But let me tell it from the beginning. I took a basket of figs to Father, just as you told me to do. But he was not at the workers' camp. He and the other stonemasons were still working inside the tomb of Queen Nefertari. Of course, I could not go there, because the place of the tomb is secret. So I waited at the camp for Father. While I waited, I practiced writing in the smooth sand with a sharp stick.

Then a dark shadow fell across me. It was the shadow of the master artist, Ani. He stood nearby and watched me work. "You write well," he said. "The lines you draw are strong and sure."

"Someday I will be a good scribe," I said. "I practice whenever I can. But most of all I want to be a master artist like you, Ani."

He smiled. "Come, I'll take you to the hidden

The artist made a grid so I could practice drawing.

I held the stone while the artist drew outlines on the wall.

tomb of the queen. You must begin to learn."

He took me to the tomb and led me inside. Oh, the wonderful things I saw there, Mother! Artists were covering every wall with pictures. There were paintings and carvings of the gods and of the beautiful queen. When the queen dies, she will rest there forever. Ani told me these gods will magically care for her in the spirit world.

"We are making everything in the tomb just as the queen wishes," said Ani. "Sit here with me.

Another artist held a lamp. Part of the wall painting was finished. It showed Queen Nefertari playing Senet.

Hold this flat stone, and I will show you how we draw on the walls." Lines on the stone formed a grid of small squares. I saw an outline of the bird that represents the soul, and another outline of the queen kneeling to the gods. Ani looked at the pictures on the stone. Then he drew the same things on a large grid on the wall. Part of the wall painting was finished. It showed Queen Nefertari playing Senet, my favorite game. I wanted to smile, but I dared not because I was in a holy place.

The artist put down his brush. He picked up another smooth, flat stone. "It is for you," he said. "I will make a grid for you. Take it home and practice drawing just as you practice writing."

Father was surprised to see me walk out of the tomb. And with someone as important as Ani! Now that I am home, I will draw a picture of the queen on my grid. Then I will practice making it bigger. One day, perhaps I, too, will paint pictures of the gods on the walls of a holy place.

Statues Fit for a King

In ancient Egypt, kings called pharaohs ruled. The pharaohs wanted to be remembered. So they ordered skillful builders to construct huge temples, tombs, and monuments for them. Some of these amazing structures still survive in good condition.

A pharaoh named Ramesses II (say RAM-zeez), who lived more than 3,000 years ago, was one of the most important builders of Egypt. His workers built the Great Temple at Abu Simbel (say AH-boo SIM-buhl), on the banks of the Nile River. They carved it in cliffs of solid rock. At the entrance, they carved four gigantic statues. These show Ramesses as a god-king. Not far away, the king built a smaller temple. At its entrance stand four more statues of Ramesses and two statues of one of his queens, Nefertari (say neh-fer-TAR-ee).

In the 1960's, rising water behind a new dam threatened the temples. People worked nearly five years to save them. They cut the temples into more than 1,000 blocks. Then they moved the blocks to higher ground and put them back together. The effort cost millions of dollars, but the treasures it saved are priceless.

Giant face swings above the rest of the head at Abu Simbel, in Egypt (below). This head is part of a huge statue. Workers moved several statues, in pieces, to save them from floodwaters. A worker patches the nose of one of the faces (below, right).

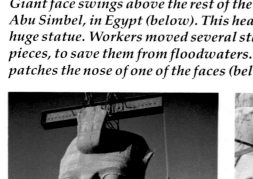

Ancient Egyptian workers finish the Great Temple of Abu Simbel (above). Some paint statues of Ramesses II, on the left. On the right, painted figures of Ramesses bring offerings to a carved god. Writing decorates the walls.

When Egyptians built a modern dam on the Nile, water rose behind it and formed a lake (left). To save the ancient temples, people moved them. Look below the water to see where the temples once stood.

Metalworkers of Benin

The old kingdom of Benin (say beh-NEEN) in western Africa was rich and strong. This kingdom reached the peak of its power between 400 and 500 years ago. At that time the *Oba* (say OH-bah), or king, had a huge army. His capital city was a busy trading center with broad streets and a fine palace.

The people of Benin did not have a system of writing. So when the Oba wanted records of important things, he turned to his master metalworkers. They made brass and bronze plaques and pieces of sculpture that told stories.

The men who made metal plaques and sculpture were the most important craftsmen in the kingdom. When they did an especially good job, the Oba rewarded them with gifts of food, farm animals, and money. The most skillful earned titles.

When they were ready to pour hot, liquid metal into their molds, the metalworkers often sacrificed animals and prayed to their gods. They believed this would make their work successful and protect them from injury.

At one time, hundreds of bronze plaques covered wooden posts in the palace. Visitors could see representations of important people and events.

Later the kingdom of Benin was conquered by a British army. For a time, it became part of the British Empire. Today it is part of the African nation of Nigeria. The Oba's palace with its posts and plaques was burned nearly 100 years ago. The palace has since been rebuilt, but most of the metalwork has been removed. It is preserved in museums throughout the world, reminding people of the great days of the kingdom of Benin.

Admiring an example of Benin metalwork, Maurice Willis, 11, of Philadelphia, Pennsylvania, inspects a rooster. It was made by pouring hot, liquid metal into a clay mold. The art of casting metal goes back hundreds of years in Africa. Such casting is still done today in much the same way, using wax-lined clay molds.

Man's head, cast in metal, may represent a king or a conquered enemy chief. The head was found in a palace in the old kingdom of Benin.

On a metal plaque (left), a chief of Benin stands with some of his subjects around him. The necklaces are symbols of nobility.

From Pictures to Words

Writing is a skill we all learn. It is a necessary part of our lives, and the alphabet is one of the first things taught in school. It's hard to believe there was a time when *nobody* could write. Yet only in the last 4,000 years have people used alphabets to form written words.

Before people could write, they drew pictures of things that were important to them. Archaeologists have found art in European caves that may be 30,000 years old.

Thousands of years later, certain people learned to combine pictures and symbols in an early kind of writing. The pictures and symbols stood for words or parts of words. Egyptians used such a system, called hieroglyphic (say high-row-GLIF-fick) writing. In most ancient lands, only a few people knew how to write. These people were nobles or record keepers called scribes. Some scribes had to memorize as many as 2,000 different symbols!

About 4,000 years ago, people living near the eastern Mediterranean Sea began inventing an alphabet. They made up letters that stood for sounds. The alphabet idea spread. People found that it was easier to memorize a few letters than to learn hundreds of pictures and symbols.

Now people use many different alphabets. Most have between 20 and 30 letters. The next time you write your name, remember: You are using an idea that was invented only 4,000 years ago!

Seated outside a temple, a Sumerian scribe, or record keeper, writes on clay. The man behind him rolls a carved seal on a soft clay tablet. The writing on the seal then appears on the clay. Seals took the place of signatures.

School workbook (left) came from Ebla (say EB-lah), an ancient city in what is now Syria. A student practiced writing by pressing a sharp tool into this clay tablet. It is 4,500 years old.

All modern alphabets come from one invented in the Middle East about 4,000 years ago. Here you can see how the letters A, B, and C developed. The Phoenician alphabet is the oldest. Greeks changed the letters over the centuries. The Romans later developed the alphabet we use today.

𐤀 𐤁 𐤂
Phoenician

Λ 𐌁 𐌂
Early Greek

Α Β Γ
Classical Greek

A B C
Roman

UNSOLVED MYSTERY

Thousands of stone seals like this one have been found in India and Pakistan. The writing on them is a mystery. You can see some of the writing above the seated figure. The figure may represent an ancient god.

Egyptian god in the form of a jackal, or wild dog, decorated the wall of Queen Nefertari's tomb. This god was supposed to guide the dead in the spirit world. The hieroglyphs stand for special words the dead were to say as they moved through the afterlife.

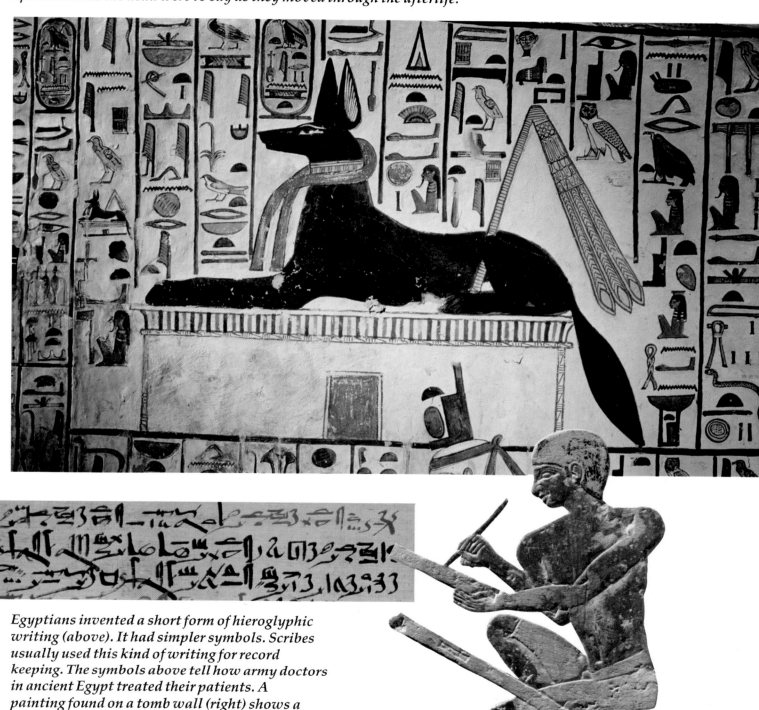

Egyptians invented a short form of hieroglyphic writing (above). It had simpler symbols. Scribes usually used this kind of writing for record keeping. The symbols above tell how army doctors in ancient Egypt treated their patients. A painting found on a tomb wall (right) shows a scribe writing with a brush and ink. Scribes often wrote on papyrus, paper made from reeds.

71

Indian Symbols

Most Indians who lived in North and South America before the arrival of Columbus did not write. But a few groups in what is now Mexico and Central America did.

There, scribes kept written records of important things for the priests and leaders. They wrote the names of cities and rulers and the dates of battles and conquests. The Indians also had calendars and written records of the movements of the sun, moon, and stars. Priests probably used the calendars to determine the days on which special events should take place.

None of the Indians ever developed an alphabet. Instead, they wrote with symbols called glyphs. Each glyph stood for an idea or sound. Only in the last 100 years have experts been able to read glyphs and unlock the secrets they hold.

Maya scribe writes with paint (right). Behind him, a man pounds bark paper to make it smooth. Scribes kept records for the rulers and priests.

On a page from a very old Mixtec (say MEESH-tek) Indian book, a ruler named Eight Deer points to a pot of foaming chocolate. The woman who offers it is Thirteen Serpent. The way they sit facing each other means their wedding is taking place. The date (A.D. 1051 on our calendar) is written below them in symbols.

72

Fingers, Strings, and Pebbles

Do you remember how you learned to count? You probably used your fingers and maybe even your toes to help you. Many thousands of years ago, Ice Age hunters may have learned to count the same way you did. Scholars have studied animal bones from that time. The bones were found in what is now Europe. Some have lines and notches. They could have been used by Ice Age people for recording things.

Eventually, people found ways to add, subtract, multiply, and divide numbers. Ancient Greek traders used pebbles in doing arithmetic. The traders put the pebbles in columns on a counting board. They moved them to add or subtract.

The first systems of numbers began with the number one. There was no symbol for zero. People in what is now India began to use the zero more than 1,000 years ago, and their symbol for it has come down to us today.

Now, we work with huge numbers and have computers that solve some math problems almost instantly. But the basics of counting haven't changed. Whenever you keep score in a board game or count your money, you are using numbers much as your ancestors did long ago.

Indians of South America had no written language and no written symbols for numbers. The Incas kept records by knotting colored strings. Each series of strings was called a **quipu** *(say KEE-poo).*

Learning the secrets of the strings, an Inca student takes a close look at a quipu (left). A wise man explains how to use it. Because the Incas did not have a system of writing, students had to memorize everything. They learned about Inca history, language, religion, and quipus. The Incas used quipus for keeping official records. A government record keeper might have hundreds of quipus. He had to remember what every knot and color meant. Each record keeper had his own code. No one could read a quipu without knowing the code.

Ancient arithmetic in a modern world. A Japanese teacher shows his students how to use an abacus. To calculate with an abacus, people slide counting discs along rods or in grooves. The abacus was invented many centuries ago. People in many parts of the world still use it.

THE ABC'S OF NUMBERS

Numbers can be written in many different ways. Babylonians made wedge-shaped marks. Romans used some letters of their alphabet. The Maya Indians used bars and dots. European numerals, often called Arabic, look somewhat like Sanskrit numerals. Both were developed from symbols used in ancient India.

⟨	⟨⟨	⟨⟨⟨	⟨⟨⟨⟨	⟨⟨⟨⟨⟨	⟨⟨⟨⟨⟨⟨	⟨⟨⟨⟨⟨⟨⟨	⟨⟨⟨⟨⟨⟨⟨⟨	⟨⟨⟨⟨⟨⟨⟨⟨⟨	◄	**BABYLONIAN**
I	II	III	IV	V	VI	VII	VIII	IX	X	**ROMAN**
•	••	•••	••••	—	·⎯	·· ⎯	··· ⎯	···· ⎯	⎯⎯	**MAYA**
९	२	३	୫	५	६	୨	८	୧	९०	**SANSKRIT**
1	2	3	4	5	6	7	8	9	10	**EUROPEAN**

Ancient Sky Watchers

If you wanted to learn more about the sun and the moon, how would you begin? Some experts think people who lived nearly 5,000 years ago in what is now England began by digging. They dug a huge ditch in the shape of a circle. They piled earth from the ditch into mounds and dug 56 holes in a ring inside the circle.

They used the ditch, the mounds, and the holes as an observatory. They noted the positions of the sun and moon in relation to their circle and the things in it. These observations helped them keep track of where the sun and moon rose and set at different times of the year.

Later, people added to the observatory. They placed huge stones at the center of the circle. Some of the stones stood more than 20 feet high. The largest weighed as much as 50 tons!

People now call this ancient observatory Stonehenge. Many of its stones are still standing.

Giant stones have also been found in other parts of the British Isles and in western Europe. Some form circles. Others stand in rows, like soldiers. Some experts think these stone constructions were observatories, too.

Huge stones cast shadows at sunrise. The day marks the middle of summer. People gather for a ceremony. This painting shows Stonehenge, in England, as it might have looked thousands of years ago. People may have brought the largest stones from a place about 20 miles away. They may have dragged them, or floated them on rafts.

Every year at midwinter, the rising sun sends light down the long passage of a tomb at Newgrange, Ireland (right). People built the stone tomb about 5,000 years ago. Its rooms may have been burial places for important people. Perhaps ceremonies were held there, too. The purpose of the designs on the walls remains a mystery.

6

DO TOMBS TELL SECRETS?

People of many places around the world buried their leaders in special tombs. Some constructed huge buildings with many rooms. Others piled earth into large mounds. Each tomb tells a story of how people lived long ago. These two statues came from a burial mound in Georgia. American Indians built the mound about 500 years ago.

I held the Eagle Man's headdress made of copper while

Little Eagle Becomes the Eagle Man

Long ago, Indians in what is now the southeastern United States built temples on huge mounds of earth, where important leaders were often buried. This is the story of one great leader, the Eagle Man, as it might have been told to a young boy.

Come, nephew, sit here near the temple mound with me. Let us find shade. The sun shining on the temple is very bright today. This day reminds me of summer days long ago when I was a boy.

In that time, my uncle was the leader of our town. Like all our leaders, he was called the Eagle Man. He knew when we should plant our corn and when we should harvest it. He led us into battle against enemies who tried to take our land. He protected us. He was a very wise Eagle Man.

In the temple, I looked at the statues of my ancestors and thought about other eagle men.

the people of the town prepared his body for burial.

When he stood on the temple mound at dawn, it was something wonderful to see. As he raised his arms, the bright feather cape he wore spread wide. It looked like a pair of great, powerful wings. His voice was joyful music as he greeted the rising sun.

Then, without warning, he died. It happened one day as the sun went down. A great cry arose from the priests who were with him. They wrapped his body in painted cloth. Then they carried him up the steep stairs of a large mound in our town.

They took him into the funeral temple at the top of the mound. There, they bathed him and painted his face. They rubbed his long black hair with bear fat to make it shine. The women wound his hair into coils and covered them with ornaments. The priests put a cape of feathers around his shoulders. How beautiful it was with its big collar of beads! Other men hung his shell necklace around his neck.

Through all this, I sat beside him. I held his headdress made of copper. A priest said to me, "Little Eagle, since you are the Eagle Man's nephew, you will be our new leader when you grow up." Then I put the headdress on the Eagle Man's head.

We put him in a long basket beside the stone statues of our ancestors in the funeral temple. I sat there for a long time and thought about all the eagle men who had lived before.

Later, our people tore down the funeral temple. We buried the Eagle Man at the base of the mound where the temple had stood. Then we made a new mound that completely covered up the old one. We built a new funeral temple on top.

Now I greet the sun each day at dawn. I wear the cape that looks like giant wings. Someday, nephew, when I go to join our ancestors, you will take my place and be the new Eagle Man.

Secrets of the Mounds

As early explorers from Spain traveled through the southeastern part of North America in the 1500's, they were amazed to see Indians living in large towns ruled by powerful chiefs. Some towns were built around temples that stood on huge mounds of earth.

The explorers wrote in letters and diaries about the things they saw. Scholars later wondered if the letters and diaries were accurate. But now, archaeologists have discovered things very much like those the Spaniards described. The archaeologists found some of them at a site in northern Georgia. No one knows the old Indian name for it. Today, people call it Etowah (say EH-toh-wuh).

Five hundred years ago, Etowah was a busy place. Hundreds of Indian families lived there. They farmed the land along a nearby river. They traded with other groups of Indians. Their leaders always came from the same families. The responsibilities passed from an uncle to a nephew.

Polished stones (top) sometimes found in Indian graves were used in the game of chunkey. Players rolled the stones and threw spears at them. They tried to throw as close to the stones as they could without hitting them. Two views of a 500-year-old carving (above) show a chunkey player. He holds a stone in one hand and a spear-thrower in the other.

Indians in towns like Etowah played chunkey on special occasions. In this painting, people cheer as they watch two of the players compete. Players wear their best clothing, and jewelry made of shells and feathers.

The people of Etowah built temples on large mounds of earth for the worship of nature. One mound supported the funeral temple. Leaders and their families were buried around the base of this mound. When archaeologists dug into the mound, they found the bones of more than 350 men, women, and children. The archaeologists could tell they had all been important people because of the way they were dressed for burial.

Inside this mound, the archaeologists found the remains of splendid clothing, and jewelry made of shells, wood, and copper. They found pottery, ornaments, and axes. They also found polished stones used in an Indian game called chunkey.

As the archaeologists dug, they discovered that the people of Etowah had torn down the temple and made the mound bigger five different times over more than 100 years! The mound told the story of five or six generations of rulers, a story even the Spanish explorers never knew.

Ships for Spirits

The Scandinavian countries where Vikings once lived have jagged coastlines thousands of miles long. Because the Vikings lived so near the sea, they often traveled in ships. For more than 250 years they sailed the oceans, exploring, raiding, trading, and settling new places from Europe to North America.

Vikings believed in an afterlife. Most thought dead warriors went to a spirit world. They called this spirit world Valhalla (say val-HAL-ah).

Ships often played an important part in the funerals of wealthy and important people. The ships were packed with weapons, dishes, and food for use in the spirit world. Some Vikings buried the ships in huge mounds of earth. Others burned the funeral ships. They believed the smoke would help the warrior's spirit rise to Valhalla.

Many people who were not so important were buried in ordinary graves in the earth. Rocks were placed around the edges of some graves. People arranged the rocks in the forms of ships.

When archaeologists dug into a Viking mound at Oseberg, Norway, in 1904, they found two women buried in a beautiful ship. The ship had actually sailed the seas for many years. For the burial, people had filled it with carvings, ornaments, and everyday household objects.

The burial ship told archaeologists that one of the women had been an important person. It also gave them valuable information about what Viking life was like 1,000 years ago.

Wooden animal head (left) came from a burial ship, the resting place of two Viking women who died about 1,000 years ago in Norway. Not all Vikings were buried in ships. Many had simpler graves, like those above in Denmark. Stones arranged to outline the graves make them look somewhat like Viking ships.

Fiery dragon goes up in flames. This dragon head decorates a copy of a Viking ship. Each year, the people of the Shetland Islands in Scotland build a ship in memory of their Viking ancestors. At the end of January, they celebrate their history with a day-long festival. Many dress in Viking costumes. They burn the ship at the end of the festival. While it burns, they sing songs in honor of the Vikings.

Vikings burn a funeral ship. They thought smoke helped the dead reach the spirit world.

Do Tombs Tell Secrets?

Royal Burial in China

Several years ago in the southeastern part of China, the government made plans for a hospital project. But a mound of earth stood in the way. It was a burial mound that had been undisturbed for more than 2,100 years!

The government called in archaeologists. Carefully they dug into the mound. After four months, they had a pit 52 feet deep. Near the bottom of the pit, they found layers of earth, clay, and charcoal. Beneath the layers, they found a huge wooden box. It was filled with treasures—silks, sculpture, paintings, and musical instruments. But the box held something even more important—six coffins nested one inside the other.

When the archaeologists opened the innermost

Builders used earth, white clay, charcoal, and wood to make an airtight tomb in ancient China. The body of a noblewoman buried inside for more than 2,100 years remained well preserved.

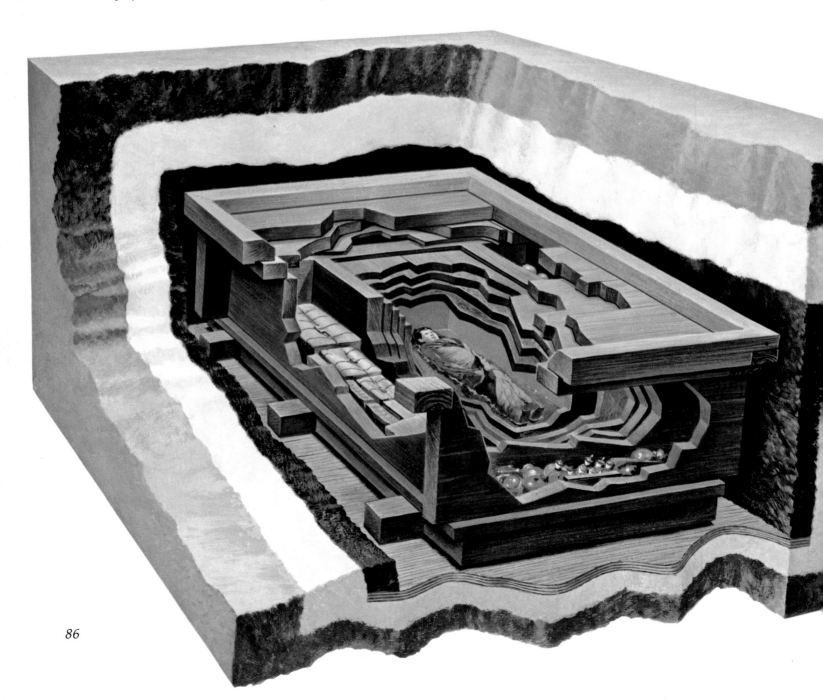

coffin, they found a human body that was almost perfectly preserved. The body may have been that of a princess. Opening her tomb was almost like opening her diary.

She was about 50 years old when she died of a heart attack. She had once broken an arm. She was overweight. Melon seeds in her stomach showed that she had eaten shortly before she died. For her burial, people had wrapped her in 20 layers of silk.

Scientists learned many other things about her because the body was in such good condition when they found it. The tomb had kept out air and moisture, things that cause a body to decay.

The ancient Chinese thought jade could preserve a body. To them, jade symbolized goodness. Objects carved from jade, a colorful and very hard gemstone, were often used in ceremonies and put into tombs to honor the dead.

Some of the wealthiest nobles were buried in jade suits. Craftsmen made each one from many hundreds of pieces. They drilled small holes in the corners of each piece. Then they joined the pieces with wire. They used gold wire if a noble was of high rank. Lower-ranking nobles were buried in suits joined with silver or copper wire. Experts think it probably took ten years for a master craftsman to complete a single suit.

In spite of all this effort, jade didn't really preserve bodies. Archaeologists recently opened the tombs of a royal couple. They had been buried in jade suits. You can see one in the photograph below. All that was left of each body was a handful of dust. But the treasures buried with the nobles—pottery, silks, statues of people to serve them in the afterlife—had survived. These tell us many things about life in ancient China.

Some of the royalty of ancient China went to their graves in suits made of small pieces of jade joined with wire. The drawings at right show some of the ways the Chinese knotted the wires.

Suit of priceless treasure (below) dressed Princess Tou Wan in her tomb. Her husband was also buried in a jade suit. Her headrest is made of bronze covered with gold and is decorated with jade. The ancient Chinese believed jade preserved bodies.

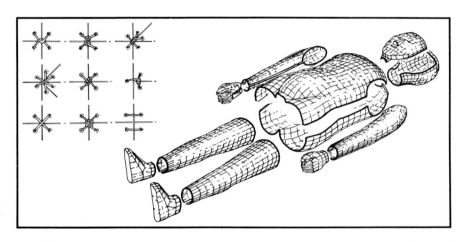

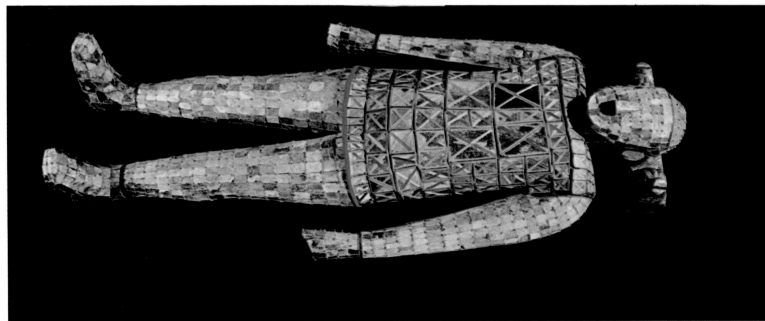

The Boy King

A young prince who lived in Egypt about 3,300 years ago was a lot like boys today. He enjoyed sports. He swam, wrestled, hunted, and fished. He also liked playing games with his friends. But in one way, he was not at all like most of the other boys. He was a prince who became the pharaoh, or ruler, of Egypt when he was only 9 or 10 years old.

King Tutankhamun (say toot-ank-AH-moon), or Tut, went to a palace school especially for princes and the sons of nobles. There he learned reading, writing, geography, and math. We know about Tut and his boyhood from pictures and hieroglyphic writing on monuments and walls. The symbols, or hieroglyphs, describe some of the things Tut did. Many of the objects Tut used in everyday life have been found by archaeologists.

Egyptians of Tutankhamun's time believed in a spirit world. They thought people went to the spirit world after they died. So they built great tombs as burial places for their pharaohs and other important people. They put things in the tombs to be enjoyed in the next life. Tut died when he was only 18, before his tomb was finished. The people put him in another tomb and filled it with treasures.

Robbers eventually broke into most of the great tombs of Egypt. They stole the gold and other treasures. But Tut's burial place was well hidden. The tomb of another pharaoh was built on top of it. Drifting desert sand covered the entrance.

Many centuries later, an English archaeologist, Howard Carter, began looking for Tut's tomb. For several years, he searched without success. Finally, in 1922, he found it. The tomb was still full of gold and other precious things. Now these treasures are on display as objects of beauty and as valuable clues to how a young ruler lived long ago.

Stairwell, lower right, leads to the underground entrance to King Tutankhamun's tomb. An enclosing wall protects the stairs from shifting sand. The entrance to the tomb of another pharaoh is on the left.

Royal couple on a golden panel. King Tut holds flowers and pours liquid into his queen's hand. The hieroglyphs around the couple give their names and titles.

Egyptians preserved Tut's body with oils and wrappings to make it into a mummy. They put gold covers (left) on his fingers and toes. A gold mask covered his head and shoulders.

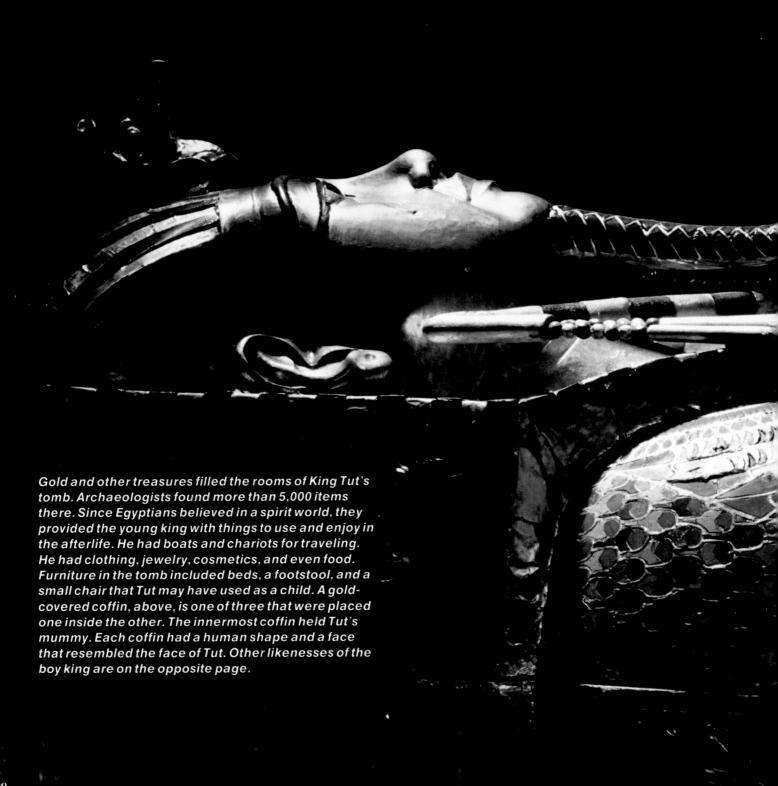

Gold and other treasures filled the rooms of King Tut's tomb. Archaeologists found more than 5,000 items there. Since Egyptians believed in a spirit world, they provided the young king with things to use and enjoy in the afterlife. He had boats and chariots for traveling. He had clothing, jewelry, cosmetics, and even food. Furniture in the tomb included beds, a footstool, and a small chair that Tut may have used as a child. A gold-covered coffin, above, is one of three that were placed one inside the other. The innermost coffin held Tut's mummy. Each coffin had a human shape and a face that resembled the face of Tut. Other likenesses of the boy king are on the opposite page.

In a statue of painted wood, Tut wears a crown with the cobra symbol, the sign of a pharaoh.

Tut carved in stone wears a headdress with two symbols that identify him as ruler of Egypt.

Wooden head shows Tut as the infant Egyptian sun god, coming out of a flower.

Stairway to a Secret

The ruins of the ancient city of Palenque lie about halfway up a slope in the mountains of Mexico. There, temples built centuries ago by the Maya Indians stand on tall pyramids. One of these temples hid a secret for nearly 1,300 years!

An archaeologist uncovered the secret about 30 years ago. He lifted a stone slab in the temple floor and made an amazing discovery. Rocks were piled beneath the stone. As he moved some of them, he saw the beginning of a stairway. Long ago, the Maya had filled it with rocks.

The archaeologist and his crew spent four digging seasons clearing away the rocks. The stairway led them deeper and deeper into the pyramid. Finally, at the bottom, they found a large stone door. When the archaeologist saw what lay beyond the door, he was astonished. He had discovered the magnificent tomb of a Maya ruler.

The Maya artists had decorated the stone coffin and the walls of the tomb with figures and glyphs that told stories. Until recently, only a few glyphs could be read. But experts now can read many of them. The glyphs often tell stories of great leaders. The ruler in the hidden tomb was named Pacal (say pah-KAHL), which means "Shield." Like Tutankhamun of Egypt, Pacal was a boy king. He became the ruler of Palenque when he was 12 years old, and ruled until he died at 80.

Every year, archaeologists make fascinating discoveries. They search the world for secrets from the past. Future archaeologists may study things we use and treasure just as we study the treasures of people like Pacal who lived long ago.

Maya temple on a pyramid hid a secret stairway. It led to the tomb of a ruler named Pacal. The cutaway drawing (right) shows the outside of the pyramid and the stairway and tomb inside. The tomb is at the bottom of the pyramid.

For many centuries, the temple above hid the entrance to Pacal's burial place. Reddish lights shine on a copy of the tomb in a Mexico City museum (right). Pacal was buried in a jade mask and heavy jade jewelry. Glyphs carved around the edges of the stone coffin tell about Pacal and his royal ancestors.

Modern and ancient Maya meet (left). Hector Aldana, 11, of Arlington, Virginia, has Maya ancestors. Here he studies a head of Pacal. The head on the far left may represent Pacal at a younger age.

7

WHO WILL DISCOVER OUR SECRETS?

Let's imagine that archaeologists may someday come to American cities and towns from far away. Perhaps they will come from another continent or even another planet. The things that we leave behind may puzzle archaeologists of the future. When they study the time we are living in now, it will be the ancient past to them. Everything changes a little each year. Over a long period of time, a place can change so much it looks very different.

Pretend you are an archaeologist 2,000 years in the future. You find the ancient city of Washington, D. C. No one lives there anymore. The capital of the United States was moved to another place long ago. The big buildings are crumbling. Weeds and trees grow everywhere. Vines climb over the dome of the Capitol Building (right). Wild animals roam the streets. Most things made of cloth, wood, and paper have rotted away. But some things made of metal, stone, and plastic lie buried in the ruins.

You dig for clues to what this city was like. You cannot read the few scraps of writing you find. It is English, an ancient and forgotten language. You also dig up a mailbox, a Redskins' football helmet, and the golden arches of a McDonald's.

Would these things be mysterious secrets to you 2,000 years from now? They probably would because so much has changed. The next pages show how much one place could change in only 500 years.

6 AM, APRIL 1, 1570

It is just after sunrise on a spring morning. Near a river, two birds called egrets watch as Indians begin their day. The Indians live in what will later become the southeastern United States. Men fish from a canoe. Boys with bows and arrows set out to hunt. Corn, beans, and other vegetables grow in fields nearby. The building sitting high on a dirt mound is a temple. These Indians worship nature. Each morning, they celebrate the sunrise with a ceremony. The lives of these quiet farmers will soon change. Europeans in sailing ships are exploring the river. Some will decide to settle in this place.

9 AM, JUNE 2, 1670

Colonists from England have built a village where the Indians once lived. The Indians moved away after the settlers defeated them in battle. The Indians' wooden temple has rotted and disappeared. On the mound, cannons sit ready to defend the colony against enemies. A fence of strong posts gives the village extra protection. The people fear that the Indians may attack at any moment. An English ship sails up the river. It brings supplies and new settlers to the colony. Other people are leaving. A bobcat on a limb watches as a family with a loaded oxcart begins moving westward.

12 NOON, AUGUST 3, 1770

The small, struggling English colony has become a successful town. Houses line the banks of the river. Trading ships sail back and forth to other colonies and to England. The busy town has stores and a church. Brick workshops stand at the foot of the old Indian mound. On top of the mound, laughing children play a game of London Bridge. But for their parents, these are not happy times. Some people want freedom from England, even if it means war. Soldiers gather to practice marching while their drummer boy talks with friends. The American Revolution is only a few years away.

3 PM, OCTOBER 4, 1870

The river bridge is a good place to watch the busy town on an autumn afternoon. A large paddle-wheel boat steams down the river. A horse-drawn streetcar rolls toward the waterfront. The Civil War has ended, and industry is growing. More and more people are leaving their farms and moving into town. Across the river, large factories send up smoke. But the workers who operate the machines earn very little money. Many live in small houses near the factories. A rich factory owner has built a large home on the old Indian mound. His daughter skips down the steps to her waiting carriage.

6 PM, DECEMBER 5, 1970

Christmas lights twinkle as children pedal their bikes homeward at dusk. The streets are filled with rush-hour traffic. A fireboat chugs along the river. The town has become a city, and the entire waterfront has changed. It is now an area of factories and stores. Most people live in other parts of the city or in the suburbs. Business is growing. Old buildings are being torn down to make room for more modern ones. A crew tearing down the old house on the mound has just stopped work for the day. Some of the workmen have found bits of Indian pottery and shell beads in the earth nearby.

9 PM, FEBRUARY 6, 2070

On a snowy winter evening in the 21st century, a tour bus brings visitors to see a curiosity from the past. Archaeologists have dug into the Indian mound. As they dug, they found many things the Indians had used. They uncovered steps that once led to the top of the mound. They found the post holes of the temple that stood on top. After the archaeologists had learned all they could, workers built a copy of the temple. A giant plastic bubble protects the temple and the mound from the weather. A museum at the base of the mound displays objects archaeologists found during their excavations.

INDEX

Bold type refers to illustrations; regular type refers to text.

Consultants

Dr. George E. Stuart, Staff Archaeologist, National Geographic Society, *Chief Consultant*
Dr. Glenn O. Blough, Judith M. Hobart, *Educational Consultants*
Dr. Nicholas J. Long, *Consulting Psychologist*

The Special Publications and School Services Division is grateful to the individuals, organizations, and agencies named or quoted in the text and to the individuals cited here for their generous assistance: James P. Anderson, Site Superintendent, Cahokia Mounds State Historic Site; Carlos Arostegui, Department of Anthropology, Yale University; Dr. William Ayres, Department of Anthropology, University of Oregon; Dr. Paula Ben-Amos, African Section, University Museum, University of Pennsylvania; Connie Bodner, Laboratory Director, FAI-270 Archaeological Mitigation Project, Columbia, Illinois; Dr. John B. Carlson, Director, Center for Archaeoastronomy, University of Maryland; Paul A. Clifford, Duke University Museum of Art; Dr. William W. Fitzhugh, Department of Anthropology, Smithsonian Institution; Dr. Ignace J. Gelb, Oriental Institute, University of Chicago; Dr. Chester F. Gorman, University Museum, University of Pennsylvania; James G. Houser, St. Louis Museum of Science & Natural History; Dr. Christopher Jones, University Museum, University of Pennsylvania; Dr. John Justeson, Department of Anthropology, University of South Carolina; Dr.

Timothy Kendall, Department of Egyptian and Near Eastern Art, Museum of Fine Arts, Boston; Dr. Lewis H. Larson, Department of Sociology and Anthropology, West Georgia College; Dr. Donald W. Lathrap, Department of Anthropology, University of Illinois, Urbana; Dr. Thomas Lawton, Director, Freer Gallery of Art, Smithsonian Institution; Cindy Orlando, Mesa Verde National Park; James W. Porter, Project Director, FAI-270 Archaeological Mitigation Project, Columbia, Illinois; Dr. Raymond T. Rye, Department of Paleobiology, Smithsonian Institution; Dr. David Silverman, Egyptian Section, University Museum, University of Pennsylvania; Dr. Dennis J. Stanford, Department of Anthropology, Smithsonian Institution; J. Richard Steffy, Institute of Nautical Archaeology; David S. Stuart; Dr. Lars Tangeraas, Counselor for Press and Cultural Affairs, Royal Norwegian Embassy; Dr. John A. Walthall, Chief Archaeologist, Illinois Department of Transportation; Gil Wenger, Mesa Verde National Park; Dr. John Younger, Duke University.

Composition for *Secrets from the Past* by National Geographic's Photographic Services, Carl M. Shrader, Chief; Lawrence F. Ludwig, Assistant Chief. Printed and bound by Holladay-Tyler Printing Corp., Rockville, Md. Color separations by Graphic South, Charlotte, N.C.; The Lanman Companies, Washington, D. C.; National Bickford Graphics, Inc., Providence, R.I.; Progressive Color Corp., Rockville, Md.; *Far-out Fun*, pp. 19 and 20 printed and die-cut by The Manson Printers, Hillside, New Jersey.

Additional Reading

Readers may want to check the *National Geographic Index* in a school or public library for related articles, and to refer to the following books: Aliki, *Corn Is Maize*, Thomas Y. Crowell, 1976, and *Mummies Made in Egypt*, Thomas Y. Crowell, 1979; *Ancient Civilizations*, Warwick Press, 1978; Baldwin, Gordon C., *The Riddle of the Past*, W. W. Norton & Company, 1965; Boase, Wendy, *Ancient Egypt*, Gloucester Press, 1978; Branley, Franklyn M., *Mystery of Stonehenge*, Thomas Y. Crowell, 1969; Cleator, P. E., *Exploring the World of Archaeology*, Children's Press, 1966; Fisher, Leonard, *Alphabet Art*, Four Winds Press, 1978; Folsom, Franklin, *Science and the Secret of Man's Past*, Harvey House, Inc., 1966; Glubok, Shirley, *Art and Archaeology*, Harper & Row, 1966; Kubie, Nora, *The First Book of Archaeology*, Franklin Watts, Inc., 1957; Leacroft, Helen, *The Buildings of Ancient Egypt*, Addison-Wesley Publishing Company, 1963; *The Buildings of Ancient Greece*, 1966; *The Buildings of Ancient Man*, 1973; *The Buildings of Ancient Rome*, 1969; *Our Human Ancestors*, Warwick Press, 1977; Pace, Mildred, *Wrapped for Eternity*, McGraw-Hill Book Company, 1974; Reiff, Stephanie, *Secrets of Tut's Tomb and the Pyramids*, Children's Books, 1977; Schlein, Miriam, *I, Tut*, Four Winds Press, 1979.

Library of Congress CIP Data

Stuart, Gene S
   Secrets from the past.

   (Books for world explorers)
   Bibliography: p.
   Includes index.
   SUMMARY: Describes the work of archaeologists and discusses some significant archaeological finds in the old and new worlds and what they have revealed about man's progress and civilization through the ages.
   1. Archaeology—Juvenile literature. [1. Archaeology] I. Title. II. Series.   CC171.S85   930.1
79-1790   ISBN 0-87044-316-X

Secrets from the Past by Gene S. Stuart
PUBLISHED BY THE NATIONAL GEOGRAPHIC SOCIETY
Robert E. Doyle, *President;* Melvin M. Payne, *Chairman of the Board;* Gilbert M. Grosvenor, *Editor;* Melville Bell Grosvenor, *Editor Emeritus*

PREPARED BY THE SPECIAL PUBLICATIONS AND SCHOOL SERVICES DIVISION
Robert L. Breeden, *Director;* Donald J. Crump, *Associate Director;* Philip B. Silcott, *Assistant Director;* Ralph Gray, *Editor;* Pat Robbins, *Managing Editor;* Don A. Sparks, *Picture Editor;* Ursula Perrin Vosseler, *Art Director*

Editorial: Merrill Windsor, *Consulting Editor;* Eleanor Shannahan, *Senior Researcher and Assistant to the Editor;* Karen M. Kostyal, *Researcher;* Deborah J. Ryan, *Assistant Researcher*

Illustrations and Design: Alison Wilbur, *Assistant Picture Editor;* Drayton Hawkins, Marianne Rigler Koszorus, Beth Molloy, *Design Assistants;* Lloyd K. Townsend, *Paintings;* John D. Garst, Jr., Peter J. Balch, George E. Costantino, Dewey G. Hicks, Jr., Charles W. Berry, Dorothy Michele Novick, *Map Research, Design, and Production*

Far-out Fun: Eleanor Shannahan, *Project Editor;* Pat Holland, Karen M. Kostyal, *Researchers;* Leslie Allen, Gene S. Stuart, *Writers;* Paul M. Breeden, *Cover Artist;* Roz Schanzer, *Games Artist*

Engraving, Printing, and Product Manufacture: Robert W. Messer, *Manager;* George V. White, *Production Manager;* Raja D. Murshed, June L. Graham, Christine A. Roberts, Richard A. McClure, *Assistant Production Managers;* David V. Showers, *Production Assistant*

Staff Assistants: Debra A. Antonini, Barbara Bricks, Jane H. Buxton, Rosamund Garner, Nancy J. Harvey, Jane M. Holloway, Joan Hurst, Suzanne J. Jacobson, Cleo Petroff, Katheryn M. Slocum, Suzanne Venino

Interns: Molly Campbell, Sara A. Grosvenor, Amy E. Metcalfe, Kit Pancoast, Leslie Patton, Lynda S. Petrini, James D. Root

Market Research: Joe Fowler, Douglas Dietsch, Patrick Fowler, Karen A. Geiger, Meg McElligott

Index: Jolene M. Blozis

COVER: Coffin of gold held the mummy of King Tutankhamun of Egypt. The boy king's secret tomb lay undiscovered for more than 3,300 years.

ILLUSTRATIONS CREDITS
Bates Littlehales, NGS (1, 20 left, 20 center, 21, 21 inset, 54-55); Jonathan Blair, Woodfin Camp, Inc. (2-3); George Holton, Photo Researchers, Inc. (4-5, 88); John G. Ross, Egyptian Museum, Cairo (6); John G. Ross, Photo Researchers, Inc., Egyptian Museum, Cairo (91 left, 91 center); Victor R. Boswell, Jr., NGS (6-7, 71 lower right); Lloyd K. Townsend (8-9, 24-25, 30-31, 32-33, 44-45, 48-49, 64-65, 80-81, 94-95 original concept courtesy the MGM film, *Logan's Run* © 1976 Metro-Goldwyn-Mayer Inc., 96-97 upper, 96-97 lower, 98-99 upper, 98-99 lower, 100-101 upper, 100-101 lower); W. E. Garrett, NGS (10-11, 42-43); Geographic Art (12, 28 upper, 31, 37 lower, 46, 70 lower center, 75 lower); Otis Imboden, NGS (13, 18 upper, 33 center, 33 lower, 49, 59, 60); Otis Imboden, NGS, St. Louis Museum of Science & Natural History (17 upper, 82 upper, 82 lower left, 82 lower center); Otis Imboden, NGS, Maine State Museum (37 upper, 37 center); Otis Imboden, NGS, Duke University Museum of Art (56 right); Otis Imboden, NGS, University Museum, University of Pennsylvania (68, 69 left, 69 right); William H. Bond, NGS (14-15, 20 right); Sisse Brimberg (16, 16-17, 17 center, 17 lower, 18 lower); Richard Schlecht (18-19, 92 upper); Nicholas deVore III (22-23, 26-27, 29, 34 right); Herbert Kane (26 left, 26 right); William R. Curtsinger, Photo Researchers, Inc., Bernice P. Bishop Museum, Honolulu (28 lower); David L. Arnold, NGS (33 upper); Charles H. Sloan, NGS (34 left); David Hiser (35, 53 right, 58-59 lower, National Institute of Anthropology and History, Mexico City); Louis S. Glanzman (36, 40, 56 upper, 72-73, 74 left, 82-83); Tom Lovell (38 upper, 84-85); Ted Spiegel, Black Star (38-39, 41, 84 right); Ted Spiegel, Black Star, Historical Museum, Oslo (38 lower left); Ted Spiegel, Black Star, National Museum, Copenhagen (38 center); John M. Keshishian, M.D. (46-47); W. Robert Moore, NGS (47 upper); Paolo Koch, Photo Researchers, Inc. (47 lower); Peter V. Bianchi (50-51, 52); Lee E. Battaglia, NGS (51 upper, 51 lower); Walter Meayers Edwards, NGS (52-53); Adam Woolfitt, Susan Griggs Agency (53 left, 77); Adam Woolfitt (85); Lee Boltin, National Museum of Anthropology and Archaeology, Lima (54 left); Tom McHugh, Photo Researchers, Inc., Museo "Oro del Peru" (54 right); Loren McIntyre, Museo Amano, Lima (56 upper, 56 lower left, 56 lower center, 74 right); Loren McIntyre, Museum and Institute of Archaeology, University of San Antonio, Abad, Cuzco (57 upper); Loren McIntyre, Woodfin Camp and Associates (57 lower); George E. Stuart, NGS (58-59 upper, 72); David Alan Harvey (61); Marcus Brooke, Susan Griggs Agency (62-63); Georg Gerster (66 left); Georg Gerster, Photo Researchers, Inc. (66 right); Robert W. Nicholson, NGS (66-67 upper, 66-67 lower); H. M. Herget (70 upper); National Museum Aleppo, Gianni Tortolli (70 center); James P. Blair, NGS (70 right); Brian Brake, Rapho/Photo Researchers, Inc. (71 upper, 90-91, Egyptian Museum, Cairo); Robert E. Allnutt, NGS, from the Edwin Smith Surgical Papyrus, New York Academy of Medicine Library (71 lower left); James L. Stanfield, NGS (75 upper); Brian Hope-Taylor (76); Robert S. Oakes, NGS, Georgia Department of Natural Resources (78-79); Norwegian Information Service in the United States (84 left); Davis Meltzer (86-87); The MacQuitty International Collection (87 upper); Times Newspapers/Robert Harding Picture Library (87 lower); George Rainbird/Robert Harding Picture Library, Egyptian Museum, Cairo (89 upper, 91 right); Kodansha Ltd., Tokyo, Egyptian Museum, Cairo (89 lower); Joseph H. Bailey, NGS (92 lower); B. Anthony Stewart, NGS, National Institute of Anthropology and History, Mexico City (93).

Cover: Kodansha Ltd., Tokyo, Egyptian Museum, Cairo
Front Endsheet: Geographic Art, NGS
Wall Poster: Kodansha Ltd., Tokyo, Egyptian Museum, Cairo
Gameboard: The rules of the *Senet* game and the design on the board are derived from those reconstructed from ancient sources by Timothy Kendall, Department of Egyptian Art, Museum of Fine Arts, Boston, and published in 1978 by the Kirk Game Co., Box 478, Belmont, MA 02178, as "Passing through the Netherworld: the Meaning and Play of *Senet*, an Ancient Egyptian Funerary Game."

Far-out Fun: *Cover:* Victor R. Boswell, Jr., NGS, photograph, Paul M. Breeden, art; Roz Schanzer (all except front cover, back cover, and pages 19-20); Loren McIntyre (19); *Back Cover:* Otis Imboden, NGS (top left, middle left, bottom center); W. R. Moore (top center); Robert Harding Picture Library (top right, middle right); William R. Curtsinger, Photo Researchers, Inc. (middle); George E. Stuart, NGS (bottom left); Robert S. Oakes, NGS (bottom right).